Getting It Through My Thick Skull

Why I Stayed,
What I Learned,
and What Millions
of People Involved with Sociopaths
Need to Know

MARY JO BUTTAFUOCO
with Julie McCarron

Health Communications, Inc.
Deerfield Beach, Florida

www.hcibooks.com

Library of Congress Cataloging-in-Publication Data

Buttafuoco, Mary Jo.
   Getting it through my thick skull : why I stayed, what I learned, and what millions of people involved with sociopaths need to know / Mary Jo Buttafuoco with Julie McCarron.
   p. cm.
   ISBN-13: 978-0-7573-1372-1
   ISBN-10: 0-7573-1372-8
   1. Buttafuoco, Mary Jo.   2. Buttafuoco, Mary Jo—Marriage.
3. Buttafuoco, Mary Jo—Family.   4. Buttafuoco, Joey.   5. Antisocial personality disorders—United States—Case studies.   6. Attempted murder—New York (State)—Long Island—Case studies.   I. McCarron, Julie.   II. Title.
   CT275.B83765A3 2009
   362.196'858200922—dc22

                                                                2009019951

HCI, its logos, and marks are trademarks of Health Communications, Inc.

Publisher: Health Communications, Inc.
            3201 S.W. 15th Street
            Deerfield Beach, FL 33442–8190

Cover art and photography by StuArt Digital Inc., Chatsworth, CA, www.stuartdigital.net
Mary Jo's makeup by Martine Tendler
Interior design and formatting by Dawn Von Strolley Grove

For Paul and Jessica

"I did then what I knew then,
but when I knew better
I did better."

—Maya Angelou

CONTENTS

INTRODUCTION

Joey Buttafuoco is a sociopath. There, I said it. Sad but true. The man who stole my heart in high school—whose large, hardworking Italian family embraced me, who constantly professed undying love and devotion, with whom I shared a million happy, fun times—is a sociopath. I loved my husband with all my heart, raised two great children with him, and fully expected that we would grow old together in our beautiful waterfront home on Long Island, surrounded by family and close friends. I stood steadfast next to this man, ferociously defending him for years after the infamous shooting by Amy Fisher turned our last name into a worldwide punch line. This same man is also the walking, talking dictionary definition of a clinical sociopath. This was a recent, life-changing realization for me—and goes a long way toward answering the one question that seems to fascinate the public more than any other: *Why did she stay for so long?* It's clear to me now: I was in thrall for almost thirty years to a sociopath.

Ironically enough, it was our son, Paul, who brought this inescapable truth to my attention. Two years ago, on Father's Day 2007, my son and I were discussing Joey's latest embarrassing stunt—a highly publicized, entirely fake "re-union" between him and Amy Fisher, in which they held hands, kissed for the cameras, and claimed they were "getting back to-gether." Joey and I were no longer married, but his actions con-tinued to affect us all. I could only shake my head and wonder, as I had countless times over the years, *When is he going to grow up? Why is he making such a fool of himself? When will he ever get it?*

"Never," Paul said flatly. "He's never going to get it. He's a sociopath."

My first reaction was denial. "Sociopath" is a scary-sounding word. I thought a sociopath was a crazy person, a nut job, someone who couldn't function in society, or a charming but cold-blooded killer. The word has been used so often to casu-ally describe extreme cases—like O. J. Simpson, Scott Peter-son, and Ted Bundy—that the true nature and scope of its meaning eluded me. But Paul's calm certainty and the discus-sion that followed nagged at me long after we moved on to other topics. The word reverberated in the back of my mind for the rest of the day. Late that night, when all our company had gone home, I went to my computer and Googled the words "sociopath traits." In less than a second, up popped a huge list of articles. I clicked on the very first link: "The So-ciopathic Style: A Checklist," developed by Dr. Robert Hare, coauthor of *Snakes in Suits*, and read this list of traits:

✓ Glibness and superficial charm
✓ Grandiose self-worth
✓ Need for stimulation/prone to boredom
✓ Pathological lying
✓ Conning and manipulative
✓ Lack of remorse or guilt
✓ Shallow affect
✓ Callousness and lack of empathy
✓ Parasitic lifestyle
✓ Poor behavioral controls
✓ Promiscuous sexual behavior
✓ Early behavioral problems
✓ Lack of realistic, long-term goals
✓ Impulsivity
✓ Irresponsibility
✓ Failure to accept responsibility for actions
✓ Many short-term marital relationships
✓ Juvenile delinquency
✓ Revocation of condition release
✓ Criminal versatility

There he was: Joey Buttafuoco described to a T. And just like that, the lights went on. This information was the missing piece to an infuriating puzzle I'd been trying to solve for decades: What was wrong with Joey? Why couldn't I fix it? Why was our marriage in such constant turmoil? Why was I continually off-balance and bewildered? Suddenly, I saw my whole life through an entirely new prism. This knowledge was one of the most earthshaking revelations of my life—and, believe me, I've had quite a few surprises along the way.

My son's disclosure started me down a new and fascinating path. Since that night, I've done a great deal of reading, conducted lots of research, and talked to several experts on the subject. This type of personality disorder can manifest itself in a number of ways. Many sociopaths wreak so much havoc that their true underlying condition remains hidden for a very long time, if not a lifetime. Of course, people have affairs and cheat on their spouses every day. Lots of men and women struggle with drug or alcohol addiction. All kinds of adults are irresponsible, or liars, or manipulative, or charming enough to talk their way out of anything. None of these characteristics on their own mean anything other than what's there on the surface for all to see.

But twenty-two years of all of these behaviors in tandem established a pretty convincing pattern. There were plenty of warning signs along the way, if only I'd known what I was looking for. Living with a sociopath disrupts every part of normal life—sex, money, parenting, employment—and I scrambled around for twenty years trying to patch up all of those areas, never once realizing that there was a bigger problem. "Why can't you get it through that thick Irish skull of yours?" was my mother's constant refrain when I was defiant teenager. She bemoaned my thick Irish skull so often that it became a running family joke. My grandfather used to commiserate with my mother when she was at the end of her rope with me: "What's the sense of being Irish if you can't be thick?"

After years of grief and worry, not to mention a bullet to the head, I finally did get it through my thick skull. I'm quite clear about what was really going on with my ex-husband and former marriage. But I might have been saved all those years of doubting myself and hoping against all hope that things would change if I'd just been in possession of the knowledge and information I have now!

This knowledge was so life-changing for me that I decided to write this book to try to help educate others about sociopathic behavior, using my own painful past as a prime illustration of a long marriage to one specific type. The list of sociopathic traits given above is an accurate description of what I lived with for years, and through my recounting of the Amy Fisher circus, plus other, more private moments between Joey and me, I will show you just how insidiously they were put into practice and how well they can be masked—especially when there's a willing victim. This is a key element in the life of any sociopath: a willing partner. Whether that partnership is a long-term relationship or only the passing illusion of partnership projected by the sociopath to further his or her goals, a sociopath is never completely alone. Like the first part of the word (socio, from the Latin *socius*, or companion) says, the sociopath only comes to power out in society, and their greatest skill in life, beyond any other talent they may have, is the skill to manipulate. For much of my life, I possessed neither the insight nor the strength to break that spell.

Apparently, I'm far from alone. I was amazed to learn just how widespread this condition is. Just as there was very little public awareness about autism thirty years ago, or understanding of what attention deficit hyperactivity disorder (ADHD) meant twenty years ago, the general public doesn't realize how common this untreatable condition really is. Millions of women and men find themselves stuck in relationships they can't fix; heartbroken parents struggle with adult children who suck them dry emotionally and financially; long-suffering friends and coworkers are continually exploited by those who put them into no-win situations and abuse their kindness. I want everyone to understand what sociopathic behavior is and to bring it to the forefront of America's conscience.

In doing the research for this book, I have had to go back, dig deep, and relive many episodes of my life that, quite honestly, I would much prefer to bury forever. As the months passed and I worked on this project—recalling many painful and humiliating incidents, some buried so deeply that only old headlines jolted them back into my consciousness—my family and friends grew concerned. "Why now?" they asked. "Why rehash all of this seventeen years later?" The answer is simple: by sharing my story, I hope that my experiences will save others from similar heartache. I wouldn't wish marriage or an intimate relationship to a sociopath of any kind onto anyone; my hope is that this book will inspire others to "get it" and get out far sooner than I did. I promise, there is a great new life on the other side!

CHAPTER 1

APRIL SHOWERS BRING MAY PROWLERS

A bright, white light shone directly on my face, hurting my eyes as I opened them and struggled to focus. I could barely see; the light was blinding. Suddenly, a female figure dressed all in white appeared over me. She put her face near mine and immediately started calling my name: "Mary Jo, Mary Jo!"

Who is this, and how does she know my name? I wondered groggily.

"You are at the Nassau County Medical Center, Mary Jo. You've been shot. But you're going to be okay. You're in the hospital; we're taking good care of you," the woman said, enunciating very loudly and clearly.

Shot? I'd been *shot*? How very strange. I pondered this for a couple of seconds, and then the lights went out again.

I awoke sometime later gasping for air, panicking because I couldn't breathe and didn't know why. I vaguely recalled being told I'd gotten shot, though it seemed like a dream. I cast my mind back to the last thing I remembered: the girl I'd just seen. That girl who'd been at my house, some teenager, just a kid.

"Mary Jo! Mary Jo! Do you know who did this to you?" the nurse asked. I nodded my head "yes." It was that girl. I tried desperately to speak, but I couldn't breathe, I couldn't talk; it felt like a hundred-pound weight lay squarely on my chest, sucking all the air out of me. *I can't breathe, I can't breathe!* I made a motion of scribbling in the air, and a yellow legal pad and pen were produced and put into my hands.

I'm suffocating, I wrote. The word trailed off at the end, all over the paper, but the nurse was elated. Not only was I going to live, but clearly I wasn't paralyzed—I was still able to write. And I couldn't have much brain damage, since I'd spelled suffocating correctly. The machine that had been steadily breathing for me for the past few days was too slow now that I had awakened with anxiety flooding my system. The nurse took the breathing apparatus out of me and off of my chest. The relief was immediate; I could breathe again. I wrote, *Was I shot?*

"Yes," the nurse replied simply.

"Why?" I wrote. She had no answer. I drifted off again, waking to see my husband, Joey, at my bedside examining the words on the pad. He handed it to me.

"Mary Jo, do you know who did this to you?" he asked.

"Nineteen-year-old girl," I scribbled.

A girl? The police had been operating on the assumption that I had been attacked by a man in my backyard. This really threw Joey and the nurse. In fact, now they worried that I really *did* have brain damage, because what kind of girl would do this?

"Anne Marie," I wrote down. "T-shirt." Little flashes were coming back to me. "She said she . . . " I was trying to explain to them what she told me—that her little sister was having an affair with Joey. But the effort exhausted me, and out I went again.

When I woke up again, my whole head was pounding, and there was a maddening ringing in my ears. I raised my hand to gingerly examine where the excruciating pain was centered, on the right side of my head, just in front of my ear. My fingers traced over a thick bandage, but I couldn't feel anything as I carefully examined my head. The entire right side of my head was completely numb, as if it had been shot full of Novocain. It felt like my face was hanging off of my skull. A couple of inches behind the bandage, I felt my hair—or what was left of it. The tracheotomy tube had been removed, and I could finally speak. My voice emerged for the first time in days.

"What happened to my hair?" I croaked. The right side of my head had been completely shaved for surgery; I had been given a radical buzz cut. Two uniformed police officers were in the room, along with Joe, his brother Bobby, and my parents. They all raced to my bedside, and even in my condition I was alarmed at how tired and haggard their familiar faces were. It hit me then. This is really bad. What a commotion I've caused! I tried my best to reassure my family that I was all right by making light of the situation, like I always did. I grabbed my mother's hand. "You see, Ma? This thick skull really came in handy!"

"Do you remember what happened? Who did this to you?" That was all they wanted to know. Amazingly enough, I remembered everything.

◡◠◡

I was outside on our backyard deck, painting the built-in wooden bench white to match my wicker furniture, which I'd recently removed from the garage, shaken off, hosed down, and covered in bright flowered cushions. It was a sunny morning in May, my favorite time of year. Prior to that, we muddled through the snow, ice, and endless gray days, knowing that with each passing day of gloom, spring and summer would be one day closer.

I felt lucky and grateful to be a stay-at-home mother in the most wonderful community I could imagine. Paul was in sixth grade, and Jessica was in third. My days were full with homework, after-school activities, volunteering at their grammar school, and serving on the board of the Biltmore Shores Beach Club. There was a constant round of birthday parties, bar and bat mitzvahs, holidays, communions, confirmations, and christenings throughout the year, but the social calendar really kicked in to high gear in the summertime—living as we did just a stone's throw from the water.

It was truly my dream house, and I lavished it with care and attention. Nothing too big or fancy, but perfect for our family of four. The front door opened into a small foyer, with stairs leading up to the second-floor bedrooms. To the left was the living room, which was light and airy. I had decorated in blues and whites. The walls were painted and wallpapered in pastels, and I had hand-stenciled the doorways. Large area rugs were scattered on top of light hardwood floors. Dried flowers and framed family pictures softened the room. The house was warm and cozy—a real home; it was a place I envisioned growing old in and someday having our grandkids visit. My fifteenth wedding anniversary was just around the corner. The plane tickets for our getaway celebration to Jamaica were upstairs on my dresser. I had a long list of projects I wanted to accomplish before we left.

I left the front door to the house wide open to let the fresh air circulate through the house while I painted. This also made it easy to see which friend was dropping by today. Massapequa was a small, close-knit community. I'd gone to high school and even grade school with many of my neighbors. We routinely ran over to one another's houses to borrow ingredients, have a quick cup of coffee, or plan upcoming club events.

I had only been working for about twenty minutes when I heard the doorbell chime. I shaded my eyes and looked through the glass French double doors that led from the dining room to the deck. A young girl was standing at the front door. I set the paintbrush on top of the open paint can and walked through the house, removing my painting gloves one finger at a time. "What can I do for you?" I asked when I reached the front door.

"Are you Mrs. Buttafuoco?" she asked.

"Yes," I said.

"Can I talk to you for a minute?" the girl asked.

"Sure, no problem," I replied, as I opened the screen door and walked out onto the stoop.

The reassuring sounds of suburbia surrounded us: a car going down the street, lawnmowers and leaf blowers whining as neighbors tidied their lawns for summer. Noise from hammers and drills, along with faint laughter and teasing voices, drifted over from the beach club as my neighbors made repairs before the club officially opened for the season in four days.

I glanced at the unfamiliar car parked across the street and saw a young man sprawled in the driver's seat. My first thought was that these were teenagers looking for an estimate on a car repair. Over the years, people occasionally stopped by the house to ask my husband, Joey, an auto body specialist, to do a preliminary assessment. He and his brother Bobby worked in the family business his father, Cass, had founded: Complete Auto Body and Fender, Inc., located just a few miles away in the neighboring town of Baldwin. I stood outside now, gloves in hand.

"I need to talk to you about your husband, Joey," the girl began. I leaned against the wooden railing on the right side of the front stoop. The girl faced me, leaning against the left side. There were about five feet between us. She took a deep breath. "I came here to tell you that Joey is having an affair with my little sister," she blurted out. This kid standing in front of me appeared to be about fourteen years old. My first reaction to this was simple disbelief. I didn't feel upset or threatened. I just looked at her skeptically. "Your little sister?! How old are you?"

"I'm nineteen." She started to get nervous.

"And how old is your little sister?"

"She's sixteen . . . didn't you hear what I just told you?"

"I heard you, but I'm having a little trouble believing you. What's your name?" She hesitated.

"Anne Marie."

"And where do you live, Anne Marie?"

"In Bar Harbor . . ." the girl pointed directly behind me.

I had lived in the area all my life. I knew where Bar Harbor was, and she had pointed in the wrong direction. Something was wrong here, but I couldn't figure out what she was doing. Why was she so nervous? What was she lying about?

"Aren't you upset by what I'm telling you?"

"What are you so nervous about, Anne Marie?" I asked. Apparently, I wasn't reacting the way she'd expected. To be completely honest, though I acted nonchalantly, I was a little caught off guard by what she said, but I knew she was lying about something. I had a twelve-year-old son and a nine-year-old daughter, and this encounter reminded me of the times I had caught them both in lies. This is exactly what I was dealing with now. Only this wasn't my kid.

The whole incident was starting to annoy me. I was busy. I had painting to do, and I wasn't sure where this conversation was going, but I was tired of it already. She was becoming quite indignant; she could see that she wasn't getting through to me.

"Don't you think it's disgusting that a forty-year-old man is having sex with a sixteen-year-old?"

What could I say to that?

"Well, sure, but don't make him forty yet; he's only thirty-six." I was half-smiling because I was being nice to her, trying to humor her. "I'm also having a hard time believing what you're telling me," I said. I pointed to the car across the street. "Who's that?" I asked.

"That's my boyfriend. I have proof!" she said abruptly. Suddenly, she thrust a Complete Auto Body shirt at me. I took it from her and examined it. It was one of the new white polo-style golf shirts with the company name and logo of a race car with checkers stitched on the left breast. Joey had just brought a stack of them home a few days before. "I found this in my little sister's bed when I was making it! He came over during work and had sex with her and left his shirt!"

It was definitely time to end this meeting. It had lasted no longer than two minutes, but this kid was sounding more and more like an idiot. "He left this in the bed and went back to work with no shirt on?" She didn't have an answer for that one. "Look, Anne Marie, I don't know what you want me to do about this, but I'll go inside and call Joey and tell him you came by." I was calm. Possibly a little annoyed, but my annoyance was directed more toward my husband at that moment. Joey was a big overgrown kid, my number one child. Long experience had taught me that whenever there was trouble, Joey was usually the culprit. What misunderstanding had he gotten mixed up in now? This Anne Marie was so obviously lying to me, but why? And for what?

And then, because my parents raised me to be polite, I said briskly, "Thanks for coming by." I turned to my right, and got my thumb caught on the handle of the screen door. That split second would be the end of my life as an anonymous housewife in suburban Long Island. An explosion went off on the right side of my head—and everything went black.

∽

When I related the story about the polo shirt, Joey spoke up right away. "I only gave one of the new polo shirts out to a customer, and that was to Mr. Fisher's daughter," he said immediately. The name certainly didn't ring any bells.

It did draw quite a reaction from the two police detectives who had been standing by my bedside taking down my statement. "Who's that? Who's Mr. Fisher's daughter?" they asked, and crowded around Joey.

"Mr. Fisher . . . he's a customer, and so is his daughter Amy," Joey said. "She's gotten in a few minor accidents. We've fixed her car a few times."

"Describe her," they ordered.

"Small, long dark hair, brown eyes . . ." Joey shrugged. "Just a regular teenage girl."

"Does that sound like a description of the girl who assaulted you?" one of the detectives asked.

"Yes, it sounds like her, but she said her name was Anne Marie." I was certain of that.

Joey said that there was a picture of this girl—Mr. Fisher's daughter—taken with a Polaroid camera, floating around the shop somewhere. He told us that Amy was a very insecure teenager who flaunted her sexuality to get attention. All the guys at the shop certainly noticed the young girl in her skimpy outfits, but deemed her somewhat pathetic—she tried too hard to get noticed.

Joey called his father, Cass, from the hospital and asked him to talk to the guys who worked in the shop. Joey was sure that one of them had the Polaroid in his toolbox. Eventually, the picture was located and made its way to my room. "Is this her?" a detective asked. I peered at the picture with my one good eye. "Yes, it could be." To be honest, the photo was of a plain-looking young girl—just like that Anne Marie character. There was nothing about her that could be described as distinguishing; she was just another teenage kid with long brown hair and brown eyes.

The detective wanted to know if Joey had a current telephone number for her. "Well, sure," he said. "She's a regular customer, and so are her parents. We have the number at the office." Cass relayed the number to the police, and they asked Joey to give her a call. "It's kind of suspicious for me to call her, isn't it? We don't have her car in the shop. There's no reason for me to call her!" Joey protested.

"Don't worry about that; we just need you to call her," the

police officer said firmly. Joey agreed to do whatever they asked, and the two detectives hustled him out the door. He gave me a bewildered look before they vanished into the waiting room. I was equally baffled. What could cause a young girl, a customer, to do something like this?

While Joey was gone, I was briefed by the doctors and nurses and was surprised to learn that it was now Friday, May 22. I was told that my neighbor, a retired police officer, had seen me collapsed on the porch and raced to my assistance. The hospital staff had given me only fifty-fifty odds for survival. The bullet had shattered my jawbone and nicked my carotid artery, causing me to lose half the blood in my body. After opening me up, the surgeons deemed it too risky to remove the bullet, as it had lodged very near my spine. Countless tiny nerves had been destroyed, causing paralysis on the entire right side of my face. My head had swollen to twice its normal size. After a great deal of poking, prodding, and testing to determine that I wasn't paralyzed or brain-damaged, I was left alone to ponder my new reality—a bullet in my skull for the rest of my life. I kept trying to articulate just how much I hurt, but I couldn't find the words for the burning ache deep inside my head. I was put on a strict schedule of heavy painkillers to be administered once every four hours, and by the time three hours had passed I was literally shaking in anticipation of the next shot.

Joey returned, pulled up a chair, and told me what had happened. "We went back to our house, Mare, and the cops wrote out a bunch of questions for me. I had to follow their script exactly. I called her, she answered, and I asked her how she was doing. She sounded fine. I asked her if she'd heard about you, and she said, yeah, she had, it was terrible. Then I asked her to meet me on Merrick Road in half an hour, and she agreed. The cops went off to meet her—I'm sure they've gotten her by now—and I came right back here.

"I gotta tell ya, Mare, I'm not sure she had anything to do with this," Joey said. "She sounded perfectly normal on the phone. She wasn't freaked out that I mentioned the shooting or panicking that I called or anything. I don't know . . . I just don't know." I sure as hell didn't know either. Neither of us had any idea what strategy the cops were using, or why it had been so important for Joey to personally make that call. Looking back, knowing what I know now, I believe that the cops were flying by the seat of their pants. No crime of this nature had ever occurred on their watch before. The shooting had been a complete mystery before I woke up and started talking.

The cops had interviewed my entire family already, asking about grudges, motives, and any possible reason somebody might have to shoot me. Naturally, the husband is always the first suspect. Joey had been extensively questioned at the precinct while I was unconscious. If he hadn't done it himself, then maybe he and Amy had somehow been cohorts. The cops wanted to hear how the two of them interacted, and they were also anxious to lure Amy out of the house so they could interview her. That phone call to Amy marked the beginning of a disastrously botched police investigation.

LOCAL WOMAN IN MYSTERY SHOOTING and WOUNDED WOMAN IS IMPROVING read the headlines of two small stories in *Newsday,* the voice of Long Island, in the days immediately following the shooting. A strange incident, to be sure—a suburban wife and mother gunned down on her own front porch in broad daylight—but not front-page news by any means. However, the arrest of Amy Fisher became the biggest scandal to hit Long Island in ages. The idea that a seventeen-year-old schoolgirl who lived in a waterfront home in the upper-class suburb of Merrick had committed such a violent act was shocking.

The press started digging into every aspect of her life, interviewing Amy's fellow students, neighbors, and teachers. A picture of an aloof teenager soon emerged, one who didn't get along with her classmates or fit in at high school. She was a chronic runaway and had been involved in a fistfight with another girl at school that had led to a lawsuit. She was best known for dressing provocatively and bragging about her older lovers. Amy was no angel.

The police, accompanied by Assistant District Attorney Fred Klein, came to my hospital room to give me a briefing. We learned that Amy Fisher had been interrogated for more than twelve hours before she admitted to shooting me. It soon became clear to all the authorities that this was not your average teenager; she was rude, contemptuous, and not scared in the least by her circumstances. Eventually, she acknowledged that she had used the name and hometown of one of her friends—Anne Marie from Bar Harbor—when she spoke to me. There was no "little sister." Amy was an only child. I was stunned when I learned what Amy claimed had happened. According to her, she had been at my house for fifteen minutes, we'd had angry words, I had dismissed her, the two of us had struggled for the gun, and it accidentally went off. What a liar!

Amy was charged with attempted murder, assault, and criminal use of a firearm and taken to Nassau County Correctional Center. She absolutely refused to give up the name of her accomplice, the boy I'd seen in the car. "Let me tell you, that is no normal seventeen-year-old," Fred Klein said, shaking his head. I knew that already; I was just relieved that she was safely behind bars where she belonged. Klein placed a sign over my chest with my name on it and videotaped me for five minutes as I related the events leading up to the shooting and positively identified Amy as my assailant, using her picture. He needed the video as proof to present to a grand jury, as I was in no shape to appear personally.

While Klein was proceeding by the book, the police had already bungled Amy's arrest—badly. The cops had lured her out of the house with the call from Joey, ambushed her at their meeting spot, and then interrogated her, a minor, for twelve hours with no parent or attorney present. The details of this marathon interview and exactly what legal rights of Amy's may have been violated would remain a mystery, as the interrogation had not been recorded or videotaped in any way except for some handwritten notes. Amy's parents, meanwhile, had been frantic when she didn't return home that night—apparently she had run away from home several times before. No one bothered to tell them that their daughter was in custody.

Though I became hazily aware of these facts during my subsequent daily briefings, I had no idea how these botched events would one day impact my future. I had more important things to worry about, like my rehabilitation, which was well under way. My fresh wound needed to be frequently cleaned out and rebandaged. This was accomplished by a nurse who inserted an extra-long wooden Q-tip directly into the bullet hole to swab out any debris and disinfect the area. Once clean, the area was packed with fresh cotton, which had to be poked in bit by bit, like stuffing a turkey. My head hurt constantly, horribly, all the time already. The searing pain I felt when the Q-tip entered and probed the wound was an indescribable level of torture. Three people had to hold me down for this procedure; otherwise I would have thrashed all the way off the bed. This cleaning had to be done four times a day, and the process never became any easier to bear. I soon began to cry the moment a nurse walked into my room carrying a Q-tip.

I was also contending with a complete lack of balance. The doctors encouraged me to get up and start moving, and I was anxious to have my catheter and all the other tubes and machines removed. Dizzy is far too mild a word for the whirling feeling that overcame me when I tried to stand. I was physically incapable of standing up without a walker or people holding me up on both sides. My inner eardrum, and therefore my equilibrium, had been shattered by the bullet. I could not stand, even for a second, unaided. I had to be lifted from my walker to the toilet; otherwise I would crash to the floor in the split second I was unsupported.

There was no way I could eat solid food. My esophagus was paralyzed, making it impossible to swallow real bites. I was living on Ensure and losing weight by the day. I had been in great physical condition before I was shot, which was a blessing. It made my recovery much easier, or so the hospital staff kept assuring me. It didn't feel easy, that's for sure.

The Fishers brought in a high-priced, big-mouth lawyer named Eric Naiberg to represent Amy. He was faced with a big problem: his client had already admitted to committing the crime. It was basically an open-and-shut case, so he came up with a very effective defense: *Joey made me do it. All of it!* Eric, who loved the spotlight, was a master showman. He immediately began a relentless campaign to portray his client as a sweet, innocent girl, languishing in jail, who had been led astray by the big, bad auto mechanic. This defense was played out not in a courtroom, but in the media. And the press ate it up. He could have easily settled the matter quickly and legally by pointing out that his client hadn't even been read her rights, among many other problems with her arrest. Instead, he went straight to the media to demonize Joey.

The story already had all of the juicy elements of a cheesy

soap opera or a massive train wreck, and reporters were relentlessly seeking out every dirty detail they could about Amy Fisher's life (as short as it was), and by default, ours. A couple of days after Amy's arrest, Joey and I sat in my hospital room and watched ourselves on every channel. The five o'clock news teaser echoed, "Joey Buttafuoco admits he had a brief relationship with Amy Fisher." Now *that* was certainly news to me and a shock to my already traumatized system.

Joe was sitting right next to my bed, holding my hand. He was so indignant, so outraged that he leaped to his feet like he'd been electrified. "What are they saying? What are they saying?" he shouted. "I didn't tell them that! I never said *anything* like that!" It was less than a week after I'd been shot in the head, but my mind was still working well enough for me to ask, quite reasonably, "But Joe, then why are the police announcing that at a press conference?"

"I don't know! But I'm gonna get to the bottom of this!" He was practically foaming at the mouth. He ran out of my room into the outside waiting area, where my mother was sitting. "Mom!" She looked up and thought I had taken a sudden turn for the worse; he looked that upset. "You are not going to believe what they are saying about me on the news. They're saying I had an affair with Amy Fisher! I didn't, I didn't!"

"What?" my mother could hardly take this in.

"They're lying; the cops are lying! I never had an affair with that girl, and I never told them I did! How can they lie like this?!"

My mother's protective instincts kicked in immediately. Hadn't we had enough trauma lately? It was the start of a huge rally around Joe by family, friends, and neighbors who knew us personally. To the rest of the world, it might have looked obvious, but no one close to us believed for a minute that Joe had had an affair with her. His denials were extremely convincing; his arguments completely justifiable. You see, up to this point in my life, everything was very simple and black-and-white. Burglars and killers were bad guys; cops were good guys. I'd never had any dealings with the police, but I assumed they generally did the right thing, helped people, and told the truth. Unfortunately, they were not doing so well on this particular case. And lawyers? Eric Naiberg was apparently free to go all over television and make the most outrageous accusations against Joey. No one ever issued a gag order. No one from the district attorney's office ever told him to cool it. The man was everywhere, fanning the fire.

Joey was absolutely hysterical in his denials. It was a very persuasive portrayal of a wrongly accused man. "Show me a statement! Play me a tape where I said that! They won't because they don't have one! They are making this up." Overnight, Amy and Joey had become the biggest story in the country. The burly auto mechanic and a sweet little schoolgirl! It was *Fatal Attraction* with a teenager! Joey and Amy had plotted to get rid of me! He had given her the gun! Amy shot me when he tried to break off their affair! With a name like Buttafuoco, we must be involved with the mob! Day after day, the stories kept coming, feeding off each other, one more outlandish than the next. We found ourselves the subject of an absolute media circus.

I lay in my hospital bed watching the round-the-clock coverage in disbelief. Every daytime talk show in the country did shows on the "affair": Geraldo, Sally Jessy Raphael, Jackie Mason, Phil Donahue. Newscasters broke into the daily soap operas to report the latest breathless rumor or official update. Joey and Amy were the top story on every news broadcast. Editorial pages all over the country weighed in on this irresistible scandal in suburbia.

I had no choice but to confront my husband after several days of this. The police were reiterating their assertion on television, every single day. Joe screamed loudly and publicly to anyone who would listen that they were lying—he had never touched Amy—but his denials were always a single sentence at the end of a salacious story: Joseph Buttafuoco denies these allegations.

"Come on, Joey," I said one afternoon. "This is ridiculous. Why do the police keep insisting that you had an affair with her? They're not telling Naiberg to shut up! The press is only running with what they keep officially stating!"

"Because *they're lying*, Mary Jo."

"Why would they lie about that, Joe?"

"I don't know, they just are. They're making this up! The only time sex ever even came up was that day at the house, when I made the call to get her out to meet me. I asked the cops if it was against the law to have sex with a sixteen-year-old!"

Gravely injured as I was, hard as it was to concentrate or even hear anything clearly, this remark really jolted me. "*JOEY* ... Why would you feel the need to ask that?"

"Hey!" He shrugged his shoulders and threw up his hands. "They kept talking about how she was only sixteen, so I just asked if having sex with a sixteen-year-old was illegal, or what. I just wanted to know; doesn't mean I did anything!"

I was too frazzled to pursue it. A week into life with my new neighbor, Mr. .25 Caliber, was exhausting me. My body was starting to come back to life and protesting every step of the way. Ironically, it seemed that as I healed, the pain became more excruciating. I was literally sweating out the hours between doses of pain medication—that is, when I wasn't screaming bloody murder as my wound was probed. I physically didn't have the strength to argue, but the question nagged at me. Why *would* he ask such a thing? I worried about it for a few minutes, until the pain obliterated any rational thought.

CHAPTER 2

WHEELS OF JUSTICE

O ne of the most prominent and telling traits of many sociopaths is their fantastic ability to manipulate others and lie for profit, to avoid punishment, or seemingly just for fun. As someone who faced a firestorm of public anger, disapproval, and just plain incomprehension over the years from those who asked, "How could she stay with him after *that*?" all I can say is that if you haven't ever been under a sociopath's spell, be grateful. They can charm the birds out of the trees and tell you black is white, and have you believing it.

I was far from alone in my outrage at what I saw as nothing but a slanderous, hurtful campaign against my husband and family. Every friend and family member who visited my hospital room was equally aghast by our sudden infamy and what they were seeing about Joey on TV and the front page of every newspaper. "A hardworking, affable guy . . . the life of the party," one neighbor described him in *Newsday*. "Even the guys say there was never a hint of him fooling around." But these viewpoints were buried in a sea of innuendo, rumor, and outright lies, fueled by Eric Naiburg's antics and popularized by seemingly every journalist in the country, from the *New York Post* to *People* magazine. Joey was right by my side, of course, swearing it was all lies.

Both families picked up the gauntlet and stuck firmly behind Joe's story: the cops lied when they claimed that Joey and Amy had had an affair of any kind. There was no official signed statement by Joe; they hadn't taped Joey in any interviews; it was a he said/they said situation. At most, I thought that Amy might have developed a crush on Joe at the garage and fabricated this whole "affair" in her mind. I wouldn't put anything past a girl who could ring a doorbell and then shoot somebody in the head. She was clearly unstable, and her lawyer wasn't helping her. He was exploiting her—and destroying my family along the way.

After eleven days in the hospital, the doctors agreed I was well enough to check out and continue recovering at home. The doctors in charge of my case gathered in my room that morning to prepare me for what was to come.

"Your eye, which is stuck open, will eventually close, and the patch can come off. Your vision in that eye should eventually be all right. Your balance will continue to improve as your equilibrium readjusts itself. The facial paralysis is permanent, but we will continue to work on it in therapy and hopefully the muscles will relax somewhat over time. Same thing with your esophagus; it's paralyzed, but the left side of your throat will eventually learn to compensate and you'll be able to swallow real food. For now, only liquids or puddings. Your speech will similarly improve." The senior doctor paused.

"The cleaning and packing of the wound must continue at home for several more weeks," he said. I groaned, but it was about to get much worse. "The hearing in your right ear is gone forever, Mary Jo," he said bluntly. "The eardrum was shattered, and there's nothing we can do to fix that damage. You will be permanently deaf on that side."

I'd realized I was deaf in one ear, of course, but I had been holding out hope that this was a temporary condition. It's difficult to describe the sensation of deafness in one ear; it's not the equivalent of losing half your power to hear. It means complete disorientation as to what direction a sound comes from. It means being bothered by background noise that everyone else automatically tunes out. It's living with a strange hollowness inside the head. In practical terms, it meant that for the rest of my life I would have to sit with my "good" ear near the person I was with, or look at them face-to-face if I wanted to hear and understand their words. And I'd have to get real good at lipreading. I wept as I sat in my wheelchair waiting for Joey to pull the car around.

Thankfully, the hospital made no public announcement that I was being released. Joey and I were able to drive home and get inside without being bothered by the press. Joey carried me up the stairs, and I got myself settled into my own bedroom. Several close friends and neighbors stopped by to welcome me home, bringing flowers and hugs and news. In a touching and beautiful gesture, one of our friends, wanting to help out in any way she could, canvassed our street asking people if they would sign up to bring us a hot meal or casserole for dinner each night. Sixty families signed up. For two months after I came home from the hospital, friends stopped by our house every afternoon and brought us the most delicious meals. It was a show of kindness and concern that I will be forever grateful for.

Everyone protected us at every turn. The media became a constant presence in front of our house in the summer of 1992. Intrusive journalists, news vans, cables, wires, and curious crowds became a fact of life, something we all had to live with on a daily basis. Reporters invaded our quiet little community, bothering and questioning everyone who came by to visit or help. The more allegations that got hurled at Joey by Amy's defense lawyer, the more crazed the media attack became. Just getting the kids out of the house and around the corner to the beach club without being attacked by the press became impossible, and the club was the only respite that we had. Its board—I had been corresponding secretary until I got shot—held a meeting and voted to break through the fence and put a gate up with a lock that only our family had the keys to. This way we didn't have to go out through the front door and be engulfed by the media fray. Nobody could have asked for better friends and neighbors than the ones that Joey and I had.

I was home where I belonged, surrounded by family and

dear, supportive friends. These people *knew* me and Joey and our kids and our life. Not a single one believed what they were hearing or reading about Joey and Amy. Michael Rindenow, the attorney who'd assisted us on the closing of our house, offered to act as our family spokesman and accompany me to any meetings with the police and the district attorney's office. We happily accepted. He and many others stepped in and did their best to stand by me in the eye of the tornado. It was about to get even crazier.

Amy Fisher was the lead story in every newspaper and television show in the country, and it didn't take long for worms to start crawling out of the woodwork. It soon came to light that Amy had worked as an escort. Indisputable proof was right there on a homemade videotape, surreptitiously recorded by her client. He pocketed a tidy sum for selling the tape— which was soon broadcast to all of America on *A Current Affair*.

The media went absolutely fanatical. It was at this juncture that Amy was dubbed "Long Island Lolita" by the *New York Post,* and the coverage reached the absolute heights of absurdity. The latest revelation only added fuel to Naiberg's fire, so the latest spin was that Joey had forced this little schoolgirl into prostitution, given her a beeper, worked as her pimp, made her buy the gun, convinced her to shoot me, and on and on and on.

In light of this most recent revelation, Fred Klein said, "Describing Amy Fisher as a schoolgirl is like calling John Gotti a businessman," at Amy's bail hearing. Though Eric Naiberg argued valiantly that Amy was a lost little girl who needed to be at home with her parents, the judge posted a $2 million bail on Amy—the highest ever in the county's history for a first-time offender.

Given the sex tape scandal and the unprecedented bail amount, the press descended like wolves, took up residence on our front lawn, and refused to budge until police intervened, at which point they grudgingly backed up to a legal distance—in the street of our quiet suburban neighborhood.

Our next-door neighbors had been waiting to relocate to Florida until June so their daughter could finish out her school year. Their house was in escrow when the shooting took place, and putting aside their concern for me, I'm sure they were probably panicking. Who wanted to live next door to the Buttafuocos and the infamous house? I imagine they were worried that the house deal would fall through. Fortunately for them, it didn't. A young married couple moved in as scheduled and took possession of the house in the middle of the whirlwind.

Every time Joey escorted me out the front door, we faced yells, taunts, and idiotic questions from the media. In fact, reporters were all over town, banging on our neighbors' doors, descending on Complete Auto Body, trying to get inside Biltmore Shores Beach Club next door, anything for a quote. I was forced to walk the gauntlet every day, when Joey faithfully drove me to physical therapy, where I was hooked up to a TENS machine. Small sensors were stuck all over my paralyzed face, neck, and jaw, and then bolts of electricity zapped through the machine. The goal was to shock the paralyzed nerves back to life. It hurt, and the whole process scared me. But it had to be done.

Joey was my rock. He had taken a leave of absence from his job to stay home full-time and care for the kids and me. Fortunately, it was a family business with my father-in-law at the helm, so the paychecks continued. Cass's main concern, of course, was that I get well. Joey cooked breakfast, washed dishes, packed lunches, grocery shopped, cleaned the house, did laundry, and drove the kids around without a complaint. He was also my nurse: cleaning my wound, refilling my prescriptions, sitting at my side during physical therapy, helping me walk, bathing me, and monitoring visits from my friends. He never wavered in his denials that he'd had nothing to do with Amy Fisher and that she was crazy. Everything he was saying made sense. It was the two of us against the world. Even massive amounts of painkillers didn't dull my rage at this kid who'd tried to kill me and the public servants who were willfully destroying my husband's reputation.

One afternoon, I endured a particularly grueling session on the medieval torture machine. The reporters outside were especially rude and aggressive; I did my best to ignore their shouts as we slowly exited the car. Joey and I ascended the stairs—a painful ten-minute ordeal that left me exhausted and shaking from the effort of balancing. As I hobbled to my bed, I caught sight of myself in the full-length mirror and gasped. I walked toward my reflection and really looked at myself hard, head to toe. I weighed eighty-nine pounds—twenty pounds had vanished due to my liquid diet. My hair was completely shorn off and just starting to grow back in uneven patches. I was so emaciated that I looked like a little boy. A patch still covered my eye, and the bullet wound was heavily bandaged. I clutched the dresser for support and peered even closer. Loose skin drooped from the injured side of my face—the frozen half. I was virtually unrecognizable from the pretty, vital woman I'd been just a month before.

This is what Amy Fisher had done to me. I was literally fighting for my life. Meanwhile, the entire world wanted to tune in to the Joey and Amy soap opera. Poor *Amy*? People wanted to hear about how Joey had taken advantage of *her*? How come nobody was interested in what she'd done to *me*?

～

I got a big jolt when Detective Marty Alger called me at home one day as I rested in bed. There were new developments that could possibly support a charge of premeditation. Apparently, two teenage boys had voluntarily shown up at the police station with their parents. Seeing the nonstop media coverage of every aspect of Amy Fisher's life, they had gotten scared about something they'd done months before. Amy had approached a teenage boy the previous fall and told him some story about being in love with an older guy and how badly she wanted to get rid of his wife. When he mentioned that he had an old rifle lying around somewhere, Amy got very excited. She offered him $400 cash plus a blow job to go to my house and shoot me.

Her would-be shooter was just a regular, somewhat nerdy seventeen-year-old boy—he wanted the money and the blow job, but he was no criminal. He had no intention of following through or shooting anybody. When the agreed-upon day came, he did nothing, and he told cops that Amy had screamed at him the whole ride home.

Amy soon moved on to a different boy. This new kid just took her money and the blow job and didn't even go near our house. Both boys swore they never had any intention of harming anybody; the police believed them.

Amy's frustration and obsession had clearly been growing for months. She couldn't find anyone willing to do the deed despite handing out cash and sexual favors. Finding no one willing to shoot a perfectly innocent woman they didn't even know, she eventually decided to do it herself. Amy's mysterious "boyfriend" turned up as well. The teenage boy I'd seen sitting in the car outside my house that day was eventually located after a long investigation. It turned out that this kid, Peter, had given Amy a gun and driven her to my house. He'd stolen a license plate off a car in Brooklyn and put it on his car before coming, so he clearly knew what she planned to do and took precautions against being identified. That boy sat there, watched our discussion, and saw her shoot me. Peter then drove Amy home, took her bloody clothes and the gun, and dumped them down a sewer.

These actions clearly made Peter an accessory to attempted murder. However, given his "cooperation" and the fact that he led police to the sewer where the gun was eventually recovered, he was allowed to plea-bargain. Peter was charged with criminal possession and sale of a weapon and sentenced to six months in jail. He wound up serving four months and was never heard from again.

My strength was slowly returning, and I tried desperately to return to some semblance of normal life for my children's sake. I had become well enough to be escorted the hundred yards to the Biltmore Shores Beach Club and sit propped on a beach chair outside. The sun and fresh air were restorative. Protective friends surrounded me, and my kids could see all their friends there.

One afternoon, as I rested on the beach under an umbrella, a friend came racing over the sand and stopped in front of me. "Amy made bail!" she shouted. I couldn't believe it, but there it was. Joey and I returned to the house and called Klein's office. We learned that Eric Naiburg had raised the exorbitant money by having Amy sign over the rights to her story for book and television deals. Amy would be released from jail and into her parents' custody the next day. I was granted an immediate court order against Amy Fisher that barred her from coming anywhere near me or my house, but the police insisted I wear a panic-button alarm around my neck at all times that would alert them immediately should she show up.

It was no fun hearing from various neighbors and acquaintances how Amy was all over town. She was seen trying on dresses at the Sunrise Mall and dining with her mother and Eric Naiburg at Il Classico. Hearing about these sightings only fed my anger. What was she doing out and about, enjoying life, while I was struggling to stand up straight and walk across my bedroom without a cane?

The wheels of justice continued to grind behind the scenes. I was living for my day in court. I couldn't wait for Amy's case to be tried and tell the world what had really happened that day. No struggle, no argument, no accident—this girl had tried to murder me, and I was ready, willing, and able to testify to that at her trial. But the police and district attorney had no intention of letting all the details of the sloppy police work come out in a public trial. In a desperate attempt at a Cover Your Ass Move, Assistant District Attorney Klein broke the news to me in a personal meeting that "for my sake" they were going to let Amy plead out to a much lesser charge. They were arranging this so I wouldn't be put through an exhausting trial. How nice of them.

They were offering Amy a deal: five to fifteen years in return for pleading guilty to one count of aggravated assault. *Aggravated assault?* She tried to assassinate me in front of my own home! Were they crazy? Here was the kicker: as part of her deal, she agreed to testify that Joey had sex with her when she was still sixteen. They had to get that in there somehow, of course. They couldn't just punish her for the crime she'd committed; they were determined to get Joey, too.

"Are we still on that bullshit?" I screamed at Fred Klein. "She's a liar—she's lied about everything! She's crazy—she tried to kill me! She'd been trying for months! She was a working call girl—this is no innocent kid! How can you do this to me and my family?" I stood up shakily and slammed my hands down on the desk.

Michael Rindenow tried to calm me down. "Take it easy, Mary Jo," he said, and reached over to guide me back down to my seat.

"I won't take it easy! What part of 'This girl is a dangerous nut job' don't you guys get? You're going to take the word of this little lunatic that they had sex when she was sixteen? Didn't you watch that tape? You should be taking care of me, not going after Joe! I need my husband home helping me!"

I fell back down in my seat, emotionally distraught and weak with exhaustion. In the four months since she put that bullet in the side of my head, I hadn't had one minute of peace or healing. Everything was always about Joey and Amy. The attorneys were unmoved by my outburst and looked at me stone-faced. Hey, they were doing this for *me*. By having Amy plead guilty to an assault charge, they explained, I could collect a sizable settlement from her parents' homeowner's insurance policy. But I knew better. This was a political decision based entirely on their colossal mishandling of the entire case against Amy Fisher. All I wanted was my day in court. But what I wanted or needed was never a part of the equation—and never would be.

As the district attorney's office hammered out the fine points of a plea bargain with Eric Naiberg, I did my best to calm my seething anger at what I saw as the continued harassment of my husband. Though I certainly tried, I couldn't ignore the incessant news coverage or the latest bulletins from the cops. They were now officially claiming that Joey and Amy had first had sex in her house on July 2, 1991. Records showed that her car had been brought in for service that day. Amy left it at the shop, and Joey drove her home. According to Amy, she invited Joey into the house where they had sex for the first time. Her parents obviously weren't home.

Now, was that a feasible scenario? Yes. But driving customers home was part of Joe's job. When people dropped off their cars to be repaired, sometimes Complete arranged for a rental car, and sometimes they drove the customer home. Joey had driven hundreds of customers home over the years. There was nothing suspicious about that. "Of course I drove her home, Mary Jo! But I didn't go into that house. I did not have sex with her. I came back to the shop!"

Matters looked a little more serious when police claimed they had a receipt, signed by Joe, from a local motel he had allegedly visited with Amy. "They forged it," was his ready answer. "Like I'd be stupid enough to register under my own name! Look at that handwriting—it's not even mine." Joey had a reasonable explanation for everything that came up. Certainly, some excuses were easier to swallow than others, but Amy and the cops were making so many outlandish claims— and I'd already been betrayed by both—that any "evidence" they uncovered against Joe was easy to dismiss.

I was firmly on Joey's side; that wasn't even a question. One night I got a phone call at home. Michael Rindenow was so excited he could hardly speak. "You're not going to believe this, Mary Jo! There's a tape of Amy Fisher talking about how she's going to make money off this and get a Ferrari . . . I'm telling you, you won't believe it!"

It turned out that the previous night—the day before she headed for court—Amy had violated the terms of her bail and sneaked out of her house after curfew. She met up with Paul Makely, a former boyfriend, at a local gym he owned. He had hidden a camera in the gym, which recorded every minute of their meeting. On the tape, Amy was seen acting as if going to prison was just an annoyance. "For all my aggravation, when I get out I'm going to get a Ferrari, because I'm famous now!" she told him. "Eric says I'm only going to have to serve two years and nine months." She didn't appear too worried. She spent a lot of time asking him about conjugal visits and hanging all over him.

She made a routine appearance in court the next morning and entered her plea bargain, as planned. The judge granted her six weeks' time to live at home and get her affairs in order before reporting to be sentenced, but all hell broke loose that afternoon when news of the tape became public. The release of that hidden tape of Amy and Paul on *Hard Copy* was the happiest day I had had since I'd been shot. The real Amy was finally out there for the world to see. Her behavior vindicated everything Joey and I had been saying for months: she was cunning, manipulative, and out for herself.

Hard Copy was calling, frantically—they were desperate to get an interview with me to run the night after this huge scoop. For a change, I was happy to oblige. The show sent a camera crew to my house, where I sat for my very first national interview in my living room. I felt vindicated, relieved, triumphant—even smug. I did my best to speak coolly and evenly and stress that Amy was a very disturbed, dangerous girl. I thought I'd pulled this off fairly well, and Joe and I decided to get out of town as soon as that was over. We took the kids and headed to Pennsylvania to visit friends. As we relaxed at their house, the phone rang with some shocking news.

My friend answered the phone and said, "Mary Jo, Michael needs to speak with you. It's an emergency."

"Amy tried to commit suicide," Michael said with no preamble.

"Tried?" I asked, my heart beating faster. I hoped with all my heart she had succeeded.

"She's going to live, Mary Jo. They pumped her stomach in the emergency room."

Paul Makely had coldly sold Amy out for $10,000; his betrayal and the immediate harsh backlash from the press and public at large devastated her. She had taken an overdose of sleeping pills. Once she was out of any immediate danger, Amy was sent to the psychiatric ward, where she spent the five weeks prior to starting her sentence under close observation.

I didn't have a whole lot of sympathy for her. In fact, I wished that she had succeeded in her attempt. My anger was still at full boil. She had destroyed my health, my hearing, my peace of mind, my husband's reputation, my kids' peace of mind, my anonymity and entire life as I knew it. I would be delighted if she was no longer on this earth.

The tide really turned with the airing of that tape; the public opinion of her hardened. A week or so after the tape was broadcast, while Amy was hospitalized, I got a call notifying me that the district attorney's office wanted to meet with me again. As usual, there was always a big buzz in the halls when I came in: *Ooohhh, Mary Jo Buttafuoco's here!* I couldn't wait to hear what they had to say now.

Michael Rindenow and I sat down with Fred Klein in his office. I knew this was going to be good. "Based on recent evidence that has come forth, we have decided not to pursue any charges against your husband. We don't deem Amy Fisher credible enough to appear in front of a grand jury," he said stiffly.

I had a smug look on my face, and it was clear what I was thinking: *No shit! Told you so!* I didn't actually say the words, but my expression was easy to read. I was standing by my husband, I believed what he told me, and they were simply confirming that I was right to do so.

Fred Klein looked directly at me. "But, Mary Jo, you need to know this. He *did* have an affair with her."

My stomach twisted, my head got hot. Something in my body sensed the truth of this statement. But I immediately pushed that feeling down. After all, Fred had proven his callousness and political intentions before, so why would he care about me now? I had too much to be happy about: Joey was getting off the hook. Amy had shown very clearly what she was made of, and she would soon be put away for a good long time, even without me getting my much-wanted day in court. The authorities were going to leave Joe alone and stop trying to pin things on him. The two of us could go home where I would continue to recover. We could return to our regular lives.

"Well, that's what you think," I replied. I walked out of that office ready to get on with my life, and deeply buried that tiny seed of doubt. My ongoing experience with the justice system and unwanted infamy gave me every reason to feel abused and exploited. The manner in which my criminal case was handled was insult on top of grievous injury. My anger at the way that I, the victim of a violent crime, was being treated by cops, lawyers, and the media lay just under the surface, and frequently boiled over when it came to what I saw as the vendetta against my husband. The only upside was that this same rage propelled me out of bed each morning and through an arduous rehabilitation. I absolutely refused to let the action of some crazy, lying teenager destroy the family and home I treasured above all else. I deserved to have my idyllic life back. I'd fought hard for it.

CHAPTER 3

A MATCH MADE IN MASSAPEQUA

Joey and I had been together for twenty years on the day Amy Fisher showed up on my porch. I was sure I knew him inside and out: he was a great guy, the most gregarious and amiable person you could ever hope to meet. This is not to say he couldn't be a lot of trouble—he was. I knew that the minute I met him—in a hot, stuffy classroom on Long Island during the summer of sophomore year 1971, when, due to alphabetical seating order in summer school, we wound up sitting right next to each other. This Joey kid was funny, a real smart-ass. He'd make sarcastic remarks under his breath every time the teacher ordered us to take out our books or prepare for a test, and get the entire class laughing. "Oh, everything's fine, Mr. Coliccio," he'd say very winningly when the teacher called him on it. It was clear that Joey was just a rascal, but lovable—even the teacher couldn't stay mad at him for long.

As the long weeks of summer school wore on, we started to talk before and after class and eventually became buddies. I had a boyfriend, he had a girlfriend, and I never gave him another thought once summer school ended.

That fall we both entered tenth grade. On the first day of school, as everybody piled out of their classrooms after homeroom, I spotted the guy from summer school across the hall. "Hey, Joey!" I shouted. "Hey, Mary Jo!" he called back. Then we rushed off in separate directions. After that we'd greet each other every time we passed in the hallway. He was a pal, the nice guy I saw around during breaks between classes. Joey was a very well-liked, popular student, not because he was a big jock or because he was the brainy head of the debate team, but because he was an all-around good guy.

The Buttafuocos were a fairly well-known family in Massapequa. Joey's father had founded and run a successful auto body business for years. Joey's mother had died of cancer when he was only eleven, and a couple of years later his father remarried. Willie Mae was a widow who owned a famous local attraction: Freeport Stadium, a racetrack on Long Island where demolition derbies and car races were held every Friday and Saturday night. Their marriage was a merger of companies as well as a blending of two families. Joey got a stepmother and a pretty cool job for a teenage boy: lap counter at the track on the weekends.

On the first day of eleventh grade, something surprising happened. I saw Joey Buttafuoco in the hall, and he looked different. He was bigger, taller, beefier, and actually handsome. I suddenly saw him in a new light. Not just a fun, friendly guy.

He's cute . . . he's really cute! I realized. I made it my mission to "get" him.

It took a couple of months of campaigning, because he was a little slow to catch on. He considered me a pal, a buddy, so I had to really work it. He came around soon enough and proved to be the ideal boyfriend. Joey treated me like a queen and was wonderful to my mom and dad: friendly, respectful, always ready to lend a hand. My parents thought he was perfect; he fit right into our family.

A few months into our new relationship, Joey dropped by one night to visit. We wound up sitting in front of the living room fireplace talking, as my father read the newspaper in the kitchen and my mother chased my sisters around upstairs, trying to get them into bed. It had been easy, casual fun. I was having a fine time dating Mr. Good Times, the life of the party. But that night Joey opened up to me for the first time about his mother's death.

Her long illness and death had been devastating to the entire Buttafuoco family, but Joey had taken it especially hard. His anger had turned into rebellion, and he became one of those kids who was always shooting BB guns at lights, TPing mailboxes, and engaging in juvenile pranks. Nothing too serious, but he definitely gained an early reputation as a troublemaker. Tears welled up in Joey's eyes as he talked haltingly about his mother and the years following her death. It was clear that he'd been deeply affected, and for the first time I really considered how traumatized he was. The Joey I knew was constantly kidding and joking around, but for the first time he had let me witness the tears of the clown. I fell in love with Joey Buttafuoco that night. At seventeen, my destiny was sealed: I would spend the next thirty years trying to fill the void in Joey that I had glimpsed.

Growing up in a family full of girls, I had always wished for brothers. Girls were expected to behave properly—at least in my house—and my father insisted on a quiet, orderly home. The first time Joey brought me home to meet his family, I saw an entirely different kind of household. The Buttafuoco house was aggressively full of life—long-haired boys playing drums in the basement rec room, Led Zeppelin blaring on the stereo, girls with coffee cans in their hair, lots of teasing, and running up and down the stairs and yelling. It was a noisy household, full of nonstop action, and the vibe was chaotic fun. There was no telling what would happen next in that house. The older brothers and sisters all drove cool cars (a perk of having a father who owned an auto body shop). I liked Joey a lot, but his family sealed the deal. Not only did I have a cool boyfriend, I got two big brothers too. The Buttafuocos welcomed me into their boisterous, loving Italian family, and I was soon spending every spare moment at their huge split-level home.

By the time we graduated from high school, it was understood that Joey and I would get married someday. Both families were in favor of the match. His family approved of me because I was a nice, practical girl who kept Joey grounded. My family loved Joey because he so clearly adored me, was good to me, and also did a great deal to help them, from fixing our cars to moving furniture. Life in our neighborhood was very simple and clear-cut. You grew up, found a good job, made some money, paid your bills, got married, had children, and raised a nice Catholic family. My parents had married young; we were just following in their footsteps.

I took an office job in the credit department at a large bank in the Huntington Quadrangle on Long Island. Apart from a few supervisors, everyone in the office was my age—early twenties, just starting out in life. There were all kinds of company events to attend: ski trips, softball games, company picnics. Joey accompanied me to every one, smiling, making friends, and drumming up plenty of business for Complete Auto Body along the way. Credit or banking wasn't my life; I wasn't looking to climb the ladder or begin a career in finance. My goal was very clear: live at home, save money, buy a house. I liked my job—the social aspects more than anything else— but it was only a means to an end. Joey and I must have attended ten weddings the first couple of years I worked there. I couldn't wait for it to be my turn. In fact, I bugged Joey all the time about setting a date. I was burning to get out of my parents' house and start my own life.

Joey's father, Cass, saw a listing for a house in the local *Pennysaver* and advised us to drive over and take a look. It was love at first sight when I saw the tiny little dollhouse, only three rooms and a porch, but set on a large private one-acre lot. The place definitely had potential. Next to the house was a detached garage where Joey could work on side jobs. Best of all, the cottage was conveniently located in the nearby town of Baldwin, less than four miles from Complete Auto Body, and the price was right. Things just fell into place.

I walked down the aisle at St. Rose of Lima Church in Massapequa on September 4, 1977, after a five-year courtship. Holding my father's arm as I headed toward the priest and Joey, I knew this marriage was the absolute right thing to do. There were no qualms or second thoughts. I had the calm, happy sense of beginning my adult life and doing the right thing. I had given my devoutly Catholic, straitlaced parents quite a hard time during my teenage years, when flower power was in full swing and I was in adolescent rebellion mode. Certainly, I always knew they loved me, but they could be very critical. From childhood, I couldn't escape the nagging sense that I was continually disappointing them and failing to live up to their expectations. Marriage, buying a house, and raising a family—now those were life choices they understood and fully approved of. Joey and I beamed at each other as we danced our first dance to Carly Simon's "The Right Thing to Do."

Our life together as a newly married couple started without a hitch. I was thrilled to live in my own house and be in charge of my own life. The freedom was exhilarating. Joey and I both worked hard all week; he in the family business, me at the bank. We were the only couple of all of our friends to own a house; all the other twenty-one-year-olds we knew were living in apartments or renting rooms in somebody's basement. We'd done things the right way, responsibly, and were firmly set on the path to a secure future. Married life was great. There was fun and excitement and having our friends over and going out on the weekends—and our very own home to retreat to every night.

The late seventies were such a fun time to be young! A new craze called "disco" was sweeping the country. The movie *Saturday Night Fever* came out in November of '77; it was the first movie Joey and I saw as a married couple. The music was so powerful that you couldn't help but dance to it, no matter where you were or what you were doing. A little percussion could turn laundry day into my own private Studio 54. On weekends, we put on our platform shoes, headed to clubs, and danced the night away. Going out was all about dancing and discos, and more and more frequently, the drug of the moment: cocaine. We were young, curious, looking to have a good time, and Joey and I both gave it a try.

Wherever I went and whatever I did, Joey was right by my side. I was crazy about my bad boy, and he in turn loved me and needed me. We were madly in love, happy hanging out with our friends from high school, my coworkers at the bank, or with his or my brothers and sisters. Family functions of one kind or another were going on nearly every week at one of our families' houses. We were equally content puttering around our little cottage, where I sewed curtains, repainted walls, and made dinner as Joey worked industriously in his garage, music blasting. He had a sideline painting flames and stripes on motorcycles. He was very creative and talented, and his talents were much in demand. Joey couldn't have been more adoring or appreciative to me. Being married was all that I had hoped for and more.

Our carefree newlywed life ended when I discovered I was pregnant. While we certainly planned on having a family, it happened sooner than we expected. The two of us were excited and scared at the same time. As the oldest of five, I knew all too well the realities of raising children. The honeymoon had just about come to an end. The young, selfish part of me mourned the loss of the life I had come to love, but we'd been married for almost two years, and this was what nice Catholic married women did—have children. Both sides of the family were ecstatic, of course. It was the next natural step in our lives.

Pregnancy, I quickly realized, was not a breeze. I was frequently sick in the early days and eventually gained fifty pounds. My twenty-four-year-old body transformed, and I felt heavy and unattractive. I no longer breezed through a day at the office and came home ready for a late night out. I became captive to the couch, swollen feet and ankles anchored to the ends of legs that used to help me race about, but which I could no longer even see or recognize as my own. As the baby's birth became imminent, I felt a bit uneasy. Joe and I had been perfectly in sync since the day we married, and now it seemed that the more responsible I became, the more he acted out. Alcohol, cigarettes, and drugs of any kind had long since disappeared from my life. I couldn't fit my swollen feet into my platform shoes, let alone dance. More and more, my thoughts turned inward and focused on the new life inside of me. Joey, on the other hand, seemed oblivious to the fact that life was about to change. He joked, laughed, and partied just as hard as ever.

When I was nine months pregnant, we went to his parents' house for a Christmas Eve gathering followed by midnight Mass. Everyone made a big fuss over me and the baby-to-be, who was scheduled to arrive in two weeks, but I was hugely pregnant, worn-out, and anxious to get home and rest. On the short drive between Massapequa and Baldwin in Joe's Lincoln, I suddenly heard a siren. "Shit, we're getting pulled over," Joe said. He must have switched lanes without putting his blinker on or had been speeding. As we pulled to the side of the road, Joe muttered something about the tags being expired or the insurance not being paid—some minor infraction.

I sighed. It was an annoyance and an inconvenience; we'd probably have to pay a fine. It was typical Joey carelessness to let these kinds of little details slide. I didn't much care; I just wanted to get this over with and get home. Joey was peering in his rearview mirror and realized that a Long Island Railroad security car had pulled us over, not a "real" police car from Nassau County. As the officer stepped out of his car and approached our vehicle, Joe slammed the car back into drive and took off.

I couldn't have been more shocked. "What are you doing?" I screamed. "You can't just take off when you're getting pulled over!"

"He's just a Long Island Railroad dick—he doesn't have the authority to pull us over!"

Well, you could have fooled me. This "Long Island Railroad dick" was in hot pursuit with his lights flashing and sirens blaring. In less than a minute, we'd become involved in a high-speed chase—me and my pregnant belly suddenly passengers in a black Lincoln Continental gone rogue.

"Please, Joe! What are you doing? You've got to stop! Pull over—he's right behind us!" I begged.

"Oh, fuck him. I just want to get home. Don't worry, he can't do anything to us." My husband continued racing home at eighty miles per hour, with the car right behind us the whole way. The officer must have radioed for backup because a couple of other cars soon joined the pursuit—and they were most definitely the "real" police. But Joe had come up with a story.

"Now, listen," he said as we approached the house. "When we get there, we'll tell them you're in labor, and I needed to get you home immediately. Just hold your belly and tell him you're having contractions."

I was too stunned to even reply. Three police cars with lights flashing and sirens whooping followed us through the quiet suburban streets of our neighborhood. When we pulled into the dead end of our street and parked in the driveway, one police car blocked our driveway and two others closed off the street. Their strobe lights lit up the entire block, and the neighbors started to stir.

"Don't worry, just do what I said. Everything will be fine,"

Joey said, and got out of the car sporting a nonthreatening, hands-up pose, facing the cops.

"I'm so sorry, officer," he said in his friendly, good-guy way. "My wife is having a baby very soon, and I was afraid she was going into labor. I didn't mean to take off like that, but I was so worried I had to get her straight home."

By now all the neighbors had come out to see what was going on, and they gathered in little groups at the edge of our lawn and across the street. I was so embarrassed that I wanted to die, but what could I do? When the officers came to my side of the car and opened my door, I did what Joey told me to do. I clutched my belly and got out of the car very slowly. I didn't have to pretend. I really was terrified—terrified that my husband was going to be arrested and hauled away when I was nine months pregnant. "I'm so sorry, officer," I said. "This is all my fault. I really wanted to get home, and I think my husband panicked a little."

Several officers escorted me into the house. "Do we need to call an ambulance? Should we take you to the hospital?" one asked politely.

"Oh, no, not quite yet. The contractions are still pretty far apart. But I really do need to lie down." I just wanted to get out of there. I walked back into our bedroom and lay in the dark on our bed, still not quite believing what had just transpired. Joe had endangered our lives, the life of our unborn child, and had shown complete disregard for our family, the law, and everyone else on the road . . . and actually got me to lie about it. And for what? What was wrong with him?

Joe rejoined me half an hour later after ushering the policemen out, cocky as ever. I don't know what he said to the police. All I know is that they didn't arrest him. He came into the room with a big grin on his face. "What are you so upset about? Quit worrying about it," he said when I immediately started reproaching him. He just laughed. "Come on, Mary Jo—we got away with it. It's not a big deal." I was sick to my stomach over what had transpired that night. Meanwhile, he acted like he didn't have a care in the world.

It was no big deal to him, for sure. But it was actually a very big deal in terms of how our entire marriage would play out. Irresponsibility, thrill-seeking, believing that the rules for the rest of the world didn't apply to him, glibly talking his way out trouble . . . What I didn't realize at the time, of course, was that I had just witnessed his first display of sociopathic behavior.

Only five days after the birth of our first child in January 1980, a son we named Paul, Joey became an owner in his family's business, Complete Auto Body and Fender, Inc. Cass's original partner retired to Florida, so it was the perfect opportunity to bring Bobby and Joey, the two grown sons and heirs, officially on board. Cass retained 51 percent ownership and split the remaining half between Bobby and Joey. We were the perfect young couple, complete with darling baby boy, loving extended families nearby, and our own cozy home. It was the

ultimate setup to a happy, secure life. It only took Joey six years
to screw it all up.

For the sake of our family's future, I appreciated that Joey
was now part-owner of the family business. But Complete
Auto Body had been well established since the fifties and ran
very smoothly, so I had a hard time understanding why my husband couldn't make it home by 6:00 for supper, and why he
had to spend all day every Saturday in the shop. His father remained very much in charge, however, and now Joe was pulled
between his father, the boss, and a young wife who was over-
whelmed by the challenges of a colicky new baby. I was exhausted and cranky. Looking back, I realize that nothing Joe
did at that time was good enough. I wanted him right by my
side, holding my hand and helping me through it. He was a
twenty-four-year-old kid who suddenly had a weepy, demanding wife and crying baby on his hands.

Between running a business, the painstaking labor involved
in his work, and taking care of Paul and me, Joey had plenty of
new pressures, which depleted his normally buoyant energy
level. A snort or two of cocaine in the mornings and a few
more at work kept him going through the long days. Sober and
miserable, I watched as Joe consumed. Insidiously, cocaine became more and more of a presence in our lives. Eventually, I
tried doing a few lines occasionally, too. I liked the drug's
effects on my bad case of baby blues, but more important, I
wanted to stay close to my husband. I wanted us to be happy
together, like we'd been the first two years of our marriage.

Now Joey was spending his scarce free time at a dingy recording studio on the seedy side of town. It's not that I couldn't have accompanied him, but I had no desire whatsoever to hang out with a bunch of local musicians doing drugs and endlessly discussing music.

Our adorable but very demanding baby had changed my priorities drastically, but I didn't want to nag Joey. What I wanted was to be the perfect wife and mother he couldn't wait to come home to each night. I figured that if I couldn't beat him, I'd join him. I quickly realized that the drug had very different effects on us. I could do a couple of lines and then stop. I certainly didn't want to stay up all night talking. In fact, I didn't want to stay up late, period. That experiment ended quickly.

But Joey wouldn't—or couldn't—stop. He'd stay up all night snorting cocaine and then drag himself to work in the morning. He managed to hold it together for months, but inevitably the problems started. He'd stagger home after a long night out with some of his new companions, wanting nothing more than a few hours' sleep. "Honey, do me a favor and call my dad and tell him I'm sick. Just say I've been throwing up half the night and need some rest. I'll be in around lunchtime."

I didn't want to lie to my father-in-law, of course, but I did it. I was covering for him, enabling him, but at the time I didn't think of it in those terms. I wanted to be a good wife and help my husband out. So I did what he asked, hating myself for lying.

The arguments between us became more and more heated.

I didn't fully understand what I was dealing with. I certainly didn't have much sympathy. The word "rehab" wasn't tossed around much back then. In fact, there was no such thing as "rehab." There were 12-step programs in basements, and that was about it. For the life of me, I could not understand what his problem was. It wasn't about us anymore—we had a child to raise. Why couldn't he just grow up?

"Stop, just stop! I quit, why can't you?" I would yell.

"You're right, you're right, okay, I really am done with it. Promise." He was always contrite, and he always swore he would quit.

But apparently he couldn't, and he was also tired of the endless arguing, because soon the disappearances started. The first time started very innocently. Joey called me from work to say he had to finish up a big job on a car. "I'll be home late, so don't wait up for me. Give Pauly a kiss for me. I love you."

I put the baby down to sleep, enjoyed a couple of very welcome "me" hours, then fell fast asleep. I woke with a jolt around 4:00 AM, realizing Joe wasn't in bed next to me. I checked the living room, thinking maybe he was on the couch. I looked out front to see if his car was there. No Joe, no car. I rang the auto body shop, but no one answered. I paced the floor and worried that he'd been in an accident. But deep in my heart, I knew. He was coked out somewhere and was too paranoid to come home, so I didn't call his parents or the police. I paced some more and worried. Just as the sun rose, I heard his car pull up in the driveway.

I ran to the door to meet him. "Where have you been? I've been so worried! I called the shop, and you didn't answer!"

"I was there, honey. I just didn't hear the phone. I got so tired that I fell asleep in one of the cars and just woke up a few minutes ago. I'm so sorry! I didn't mean to worry you . . . I thought you'd be sound asleep. You waited up all night for me? How sweet! Do you know how much I love you?" And he wrapped his arms around me in a big, comforting hug.

I was relieved to see him alive and unhurt, but I had to ask, "Were you out all night doing blow?"

"Absolutely not!" he answered firmly, looking me straight in the eye. "I told you—I was working and fell asleep!"

But then it happened again . . . and again. The disappearances started happening every few weeks or so, and I could not imagine what had gone wrong with my marriage. "I'm just running over to the shop for an hour," he'd say after dinner—then fail to come home for two days. I failed to comprehend that I was dealing with an addict. In my mind, someone who did lots of cocaine every day was an addict. Joey could stay away from it for weeks or months at a time, so I was sure he wasn't really "addicted." Then he'd binge until he worried that I really would leave unless he quit. He'd stop again, we'd have a few relatively calm months, and then the whole cycle would play itself out again.

Boy, could he ever lie! He would look me right in the eye and spin the most preposterous stories about where he was, what he was doing, and why he looked and acted so odd. His manner was more convincing than the lie itself; he had an answer for everything, never skipping a beat or getting flustered by my pointed questioning. Sincerity seeped from every pore, constantly assuring me how much he loved me and that I was the most beautiful, understanding woman in the world. He was a master manipulator, playing on my need to be a perfect wife and mother.

Wanting to believe my husband, hoping for the best, I refused to face the fact that he was a liar. I loved Joe, we had a beautiful son, and I was in this marriage for the long haul. I thought I could help him. I thought I could fix things. Bottom line: I just couldn't leave, though there were times when I really believed I'd had enough. More than once, he'd come home after a three-day binge, and I'd have my mind made up. I simply could not raise a child and deal with his drug use and disappearances. Usually, I was driven to hysteria by the time he came in the door, but sometimes I was oddly calm. "Joe, I can't live like this anymore. We are going to have to get a divorce," I would say, and mean it.

"Oh, no, no . . . you can't leave me, I love you . . . I swear, Mary Jo, I'll never do it again." These rare showdowns really scared Joe. He would write the most beautiful, heartfelt letters, bring me expensive jewelry, and make a million sincere-sounding promises. He swore it would never happen again. I wanted to think that, this time, he meant it. And he was so convincing that I bought his story—every time.

CHAPTER 4

GOING BONKERS IN BALDWIN

Our relationship wasn't all unrelieved misery and worry. Life could run along smoothly and happily for months. That was the crazy-making part, the reason I stuck it out during the bad times, because the good times were fantastic. We took family vacations to the Bahamas and Florida, hung out with our friends and their babies, doted on Paul, sang to each other along with the radio as we drove around town, and laughed. We laughed all the time! Then one night without warning, he'd disappear, make me frantic with worry, eventually return, and beg my forgiveness. Soon enough, he'd wear me down, talk me into staying, and "behave" for a few more months—at one point for such an extended period that we agreed it was time to have another baby. It was a dreadful dance, one familiar to anyone who lives with an alcoholic or drug addict, and we both knew all the steps.

When Jessica arrived in March 1983, I now had two babies—three, if you counted my husband. If anything, Joe's binges were becoming worse. The pressure of living with a cocaine addict while pretending everything was fine sent my anxiety levels off the charts. One day, I headed to the store to buy Jessie some diapers. Both kids were parked in the shopping cart, and as I walked the aisles of the familiar supermarket, which I visited twice a week every week of my life, a wave of nausea swept over me. I suddenly found it hard to breathe and started gasping for air. The world turned black at the edges as my vision narrowed. I began to panic and broke into a cold sweat. I was so dizzy that I was sure I was going to pass out, and all I could think of was what would happen to my babies if I lost consciousness, not to mention how embarrassing it would be.

I've got to get out of here! was the only thought in my head. *Now!* It was an all-consuming urge. My brain was literally screaming, *Run! Go!* I grabbed the kids, abandoned my cart, and ran out of the store. Once I got outside, I felt normal again within three minutes. I packed the kids back into the car and sat there wondering, *What the hell just happened to me?* The most debilitating wave of sheer terror had come from nowhere and taken over. I had never felt that scared in my entire life. I gave up on shopping and drove home.

Of course, I had to go back to the store the next day to get the diapers, but once I parked in the lot, I couldn't force myself out of the car. The fear of another attack kept me rooted in the front seat. If it happened to me again while I was in the store with the kids, what was I going to do? I agonized for half an hour, then gave up and drove home. The voice in my head

that constantly monitored my behavior was taunting me full
blast. *What kind of mother are you? You can't even go into the
store and buy diapers. What a dope!*

The fright had been so overwhelming that I felt like I was
going to die. I almost would have preferred to die rather than
live through an experience like that again. The anticipatory
anxiety of having another attack was horrible. I could not make
myself go into that grocery store. Not that day, or the next, or
that week. The wave swept over me again the following week
after I'd sternly told myself to pull it together and screwed up
all my courage to enter the hardware store. Once again, I found
myself shaking, sweating, and gasping on the sidewalk.

Still, I tried to keep up appearances. Nobody knew that Joe
was disappearing for days on end, nobody knew I had excruciating panic attacks, nobody knew that my life was falling apart.
I was too ashamed to tell anybody; that old feeling of not living up to expectations kicked in, effectively sealing my mouth.
It took all my energy just to keep daily life moving along. I was
holding all my problems inside while playing the role of happy,
devoted wife and mother. It was killing me.

Joe's father and brother had a pretty good idea of what was
going on with him because they saw him every day . . . or
didn't, when he didn't bother to show up for work. His
brother Bobby in particular had his suspicions, especially after
things started to go missing in the shop—money, car parts,
tools. But Joey could look him straight in the eye, tell him a
story, and make him believe it. Joey was Bobby's kid brother,

the good guy, the prankster, the lovable rascal. Joey knew just how to handle his brother. His father, meanwhile, ignored Joey's erratic behavior and hoped for the best, handing out his regular paycheck every week as he'd always done. All of us were enabling Joey, but we didn't think of our behavior in those terms. It was family, and we all wanted to help.

Paul was enrolled in a nursery school, and part of being a parent there meant helping the teacher one day a month. When my day came, I forced myself to get to the school and inside the classroom. But right in the middle of handing out juice to ten preschoolers in the bright, toy-filled playroom, I felt the now-familiar wave engulfing me. I stammered to the teacher that I wasn't feeling well. "I'm going to pass out," I told her.

She sat me down and tried to help. She was kind and understanding, but eventually she had to call Joe to come and get me. I was not capable of driving. I broke down on that car ride home. "You're making me crazy, Joe. I can't take this anymore. I'm going out of my mind. I am literally cracking up!" Grim and stone-faced beside me, for once Joe had nothing to say. He was well aware of how his disappearances affected me. He could easily see that I was sinking, and knew that his behavior had everything to do with it.

He didn't stop disappearing on binges, but he picked up the slack—he had no choice. Joey took care of the grocery shopping and errands for me when I couldn't make it out the door during the day. He didn't complain, but that only made me feel worse. My self-esteem was steadily eroding, and this gave the scolding voice in my head plenty more to say. *Your husband is God-knows-where doing drugs, and you can't even take care of your own children!* It was a dreadful, downward spiral that soon left me almost completely housebound. I found excuses to have family and friends come see me instead of going out. The planning, fibbing, and hiding my condition exhausted me even further.

In my mind, I thought that maybe having the kids with me all the time was the problem behind these attacks. That was my main fear—passing out or becoming incapacitated while they were in my care. So I asked my mother to come babysit so I could do some Christmas shopping alone. She knew nothing about my anxiety attacks or how days and days passed when I was unable to leave the house. A good five years into my marriage, I was still very much invested in being the good, responsible daughter, wife, and mother. I dreaded my mother's disapproval. I looked fine, so she assumed everything was fine. There was no way I could tell her what was really going on.

I parked my car in the Toys "R" Us lot and gave myself a pep talk. *The kids aren't here. You can do this!* I told myself. *You'll be okay.* I got myself into the store and filled a cart. Everything was going fine. And then it started again. Panic engulfed me. My heart started pounding, I couldn't breathe, I felt like I was about to faint, throw up, and pass out all at once. I abandoned my cart in the store and ran out to my car.

I would have done anything to keep this secret from my mother, but for the life of me I could not get out of that car and go into that store again. I sat in the parking lot, weeping, pounding the steering wheel in frustration, knowing that my mother was about to learn that her daughter literally could not function. For two hours I sat there ashamed, crying my heart out, willing myself to go back into that damn store, check out, and get the presents home. But I couldn't. Finally, defeated, I drove home to face the music.

My mother could see that something was wrong the minute I walked through the door.

"What's the matter, Mary Jo?"

"I had to leave the store, Mom. I couldn't stay. I have these panic attacks that come over me. I don't know why, but I've been getting them a lot. I get so scared that I have to run outside."

She was concerned, not at all judgmental. "My goodness, how long has this been going on?"

"A long time," I choked out. "Probably six months or a year. Mom, it's really bad."

"Well, honey, it's hard with two little ones. It's exhausting. Maybe you need a checkup?" My mother, who could at times be quite critical, was supportive and sweet, but the shame of living with a drug addict wouldn't allow me to tell her what was really wrong. I felt like a ten-year-old who was hiding candy under her bed and immediately started backpedaling.

"Yes . . . I'm just overtired . . . I'm sure I'll be fine tomorrow. But, sure, I'll get a checkup."

Being exposed, even to my own mother, had been mortifying. I vowed to fix myself somehow. It started with a trip to the local library—an ordeal in and of itself. "Freaking out," I wrote on scrap paper. "What's wrong with me?" I brushed aside the librarian's offer to help and headed straight to the card catalog. I looked up "anxiety" and "panic." I pulled a pile of medical and self-help books off the shelf and read up on panic attacks. They were totally in my head, I learned. I wasn't really going to have a heart attack or die; it only felt like it. Talk therapy and drug therapy were the recommended treatments. It was a relief to know, in clinical terms, what was happening to me and that I hadn't completely lost my mind. Still, I wasn't ready to admit my troubles to anyone. I redoubled my efforts to pull myself together.

That spring, Joey and I decided to build an addition onto our house. With two small children, we desperately needed more room. I was attempting to live normally and do regular things like remodel the house, even though my life was falling apart. Some more space and breathing room would do us all good. If I couldn't make it out into the fresh air, I would at least expand my living quarters. The painter, a friend of ours from high school, was coming over to show us paint swatches one night after dinner, and I was racing around trying to clean up. I ran after Jessica, leaned over to pick her up, and discovered that my arms were frozen. I literally could not pick up my own daughter. For a moment I thought I was having another attack, but this was different.

With an enormous effort I picked up the phone, punched in

the number to the shop, and told Joe, "Something's wrong with me. I can barely move. You have to come home—it's an emergency."

He raced home. I had scared the hell out of him. "I can't move! I can't move!" I cried as he walked in the door. I literally crawled into bed. "I don't know what's wrong with me!" I cried hopelessly. The constant anxiety, the debilitating panic attacks, the agoraphobia, and now this inability to even move—my life had come to this. My nerves were shot and were now getting the best of me. My body was rebelling. I was done.

"I need to see a doctor," I told Joe. "I need to be on medication because I literally cannot function anymore." The next morning, I picked up the phone book, thumbed through the yellow pages, called the psychiatrist nearest our house, and booked an appointment.

When I arrived at the doctor's, it all burst out of me. "I can't leave the house. When I do, I'm shaking because I'm so scared. I never know when these attacks are going to come over me. I have two little kids who need to be taken to nursery school every day. I need to be able to run my errands. I'm thirty years old, and I am cracking up."

We had a short discussion about the nature and treatment of panic attacks, and I was prescribed antianxiety medication. I was also given a referral for behavioral therapy, which I immediately started. My problems didn't disappear—likely because I didn't mention my husband's cocaine abuse—but I wasn't expecting anyone to fix that. I was too ashamed to tell anyone that my picture-perfect life—the son and daughter, picket fence, family business, husband everybody loved—wasn't really so perfect. That was an admission I was unwilling to make to my mother, my sisters, my friends, or even a doctor who had heard it all before.

All I wanted was to be able to function again, and Xanax proved to be a good buffer. It was, in fact, a miracle drug in terms of stopping the panic attacks in their tracks. Medication didn't address my underlying problems, of course, but it certainly managed the symptoms. I found the therapy sessions extremely helpful. I was given all kinds of tricks and tips to try when the panic attacks arrived. The crux of the training was realizing that I might not be able to control when an attack might arrive, but I was capable of learning to control my own reaction to it. I completed an eight-week behavior modification program, stayed on my meds, and slowly but steadily got out of the house and resumed holding things together.

Once I was back to a reasonable level of functioning, I focused on a new plan. My thinking was that if we left our current neighborhood and moved back to Massapequa, the town where we had both grown up, we would be even closer to both our families and support systems. I could get Joey farther away from all the bad influences in Baldwin: the recording studio, his disreputable friends, the hangouts where he bought and did drugs. Paul was nearing school age, and it was the perfect time to settle somewhere new if we were ever going to make a move out of the school district. So I began a serious house-hunt. This is what an enabler does best—tries to put a Band-Aid on the problem instead of addressing the situation head-on.

I found the perfect house for sale in Massapequa, right on the water and next door to the Biltmore Shores Beach Club. We loved swimming, boating, and all water sports, so the location alone was ideal. Not to mention that both our families' homes were only blocks away, and we knew many of the neighbors on all the surrounding streets. We put a retainer on the house in Massapequa, and I prepared to put our cottage up for sale.

Joey came home one night with great news. He had found a private buyer interested in the house who would pay cash for it. "How can he afford to do that?" I asked. Joey went into a whole explanation of how this buyer was a single guy, a suc-cessful entrepreneur, that our house was perfect for him, and blah blah blah. I met the guy. He seemed all right and gave me basically the same story. *Hmmm,* I thought, *we won't have to pay any real estate agent fees for the sale of this house. Great—let's do it!* That was easy. I proceeded to get on with the major cleanup, toss-out, and packing that came with ten years of life in one house. It was a huge job, but I was motivated and ex-cited. We were going to make a fresh start.

When moving day arrived, Joey and I had an appointment midmorning at our lawyer's office to close on the Massapequa house. I rose at dawn and raced around, packing last-minute boxes and loading our cars with things we'd need immediately at the new house. Eventually, I glanced at my watch and found my husband in his garage. "Come on, let's go! We have to get over to Mike Rindenow's office. Where's the money, Joey? The guy gave you a cashier's check, right?"

"Ahhhh . . . let's go inside and talk for a minute," Joey said. He looked guilty and nervous. I followed him into the cottage, dodging all the boxes stacked in every room, impatient and anxious to get moving. He sat me down on the bare floor of the living room, where the imprints from the legs of my coffee table remained. He then walked across the room, as far away from me as he could get, and slumped to the floor, leaning up against a blank wall. He was trapped with nowhere to go. I knew something was up, but nothing could have prepared me for what came out of my husband's mouth. "It's gone, Mary Jo. There is no money." He couldn't even look at me when he said these words. I started to shake. I thought I was going to vomit.

"What do you mean, it's *gone*? *Where did it go*?" Well, it turned out that Joey had signed over the deed to our house to his cocaine dealer because he owed him so much money. As the story came out, I wanted to kill him right then and there in our empty living room. We were closing on the new house in a couple of hours, and there was no money! The Xanax came in real handy that day as I tried to absorb this blow.

The endless scrambling around and lying had caught up with Joey this time. He cried. He was sorry. He would fix it. So he went to see Enabler Number Two: my father-in-law. His father was shocked and disappointed, of course, but he didn't want to see his daughter-in-law and grandchildren homeless, so he offered us a solution. He would give us the $50,000 that we had agreed to put down on the new house, but Joe would lose his ownership shares in the business. From that point on, Joe would just be an employee.

My husband signed the papers and we got the new house, but he threw his whole future away because drugs had become more important to him than his family. You would think that would have been a major wake-up call to him, but, incredibly, it wasn't.

It took weeks for me to recover from the shock of the lost $50,000. Fortunately, I had plenty to keep me busy. I was racing around unpacking, setting up the new house, socializing with the new neighbors, arranging for Paul to enter school, and the million and one other details that come with moving. In our first couple of months at the new house, Joey really lost control. He pulled a couple more disappearing acts, and these were major binges. He dragged home looking sick and lost—skinny, with dark circles under his eyes, unshaven. He was unraveling right before my eyes.

My mother stopped by one morning for coffee. As we sat in my new kitchen overlooking the water, she said, "Joey's doing drugs, isn't he?"

"How did you know?" I asked, while I cursed myself. I had been making excuses for so long about how hard Joey was working, big jobs, late nights—now the secret was out. It was actually a tremendous relief; the game was over. I couldn't hide anymore.

A few weeks later, when Joey disappeared yet again, I felt an inexplicable calm descend upon me. *This is it . . . the end*, I thought. I located a treatment center in the nearby town of Amityville and called to speak to a counselor. "My husband is a cocaine addict and has been for years. Can you help him?" I asked. After a great deal of discussion about Joey's habit and endless insurance documentation, the man promised that a bed would be held open. He cautioned me that Joey would need to remain at their facility for at least three weeks. "I'll be bringing him in the minute he walks in the door," I promised.

Then I dialed Cass at the garage. Joey wasn't there, of course. "Dad, we're going to lose Joey if we don't do something. He's going to die if we don't get him help. He needs treatment, and he'll need to take some time off work." I wasn't asking—I was telling. Cass had an urgent family discussion with his wife and Bobby and called me right back. "Do it," he said.

The next call was to my own parents. "I'm putting Joe into a drug treatment center," I told them. "I'll need you to watch the kids while I'm gone if you could, please." Of course, they agreed. My mother came right over and picked up Paul and Jessica for an overnight.

I was well over the age of thirty, but was finally, at long last, acting like a real grown-up. I packed a bag for my husband and waited for him to wander home. When he came in, as he always did, with his tail between his legs, I didn't yell or cry or reproach him. I sat him down and said, "Joey, you are going to rehab. Today. If you don't go, I am leaving you. Today."

He definitely heard something new in my voice. "But my job ... I have to work ... " he started.

"The treatment center is waiting for you to arrive. All the arrangements have been made. I've already spoken to your parents and mine about this. We are all in agreement." That statement really threw him—he knew very well how invested I was in keeping up appearances at all costs. In fact, he'd been counting on that weakness for many years. But I was no longer going to play that game; I had no reason to. My ugly secret had been exposed.

Cocaine was Joe's mistress for the first ten years of our marriage. To his credit, when I finally put my foot down, he didn't put up any resistance. We drove to the treatment center, where he remained for the next three weeks. Joey successfully completed treatment, attended a 12-step program, and came out clean and sober. He never touched cocaine again.

As anyone who has lived with a substance abuser can attest to, the problems caused by alcohol and drug addiction alone are so overwhelming that there's no need to look any deeper for a root cause of all the marital, work, and financial problems that addiction leaves in its wake. And I want to stress that alcoholism or drug addiction does not in any way necessarily equal sociopathy. However, the symptoms of addiction do mimic many of the sociopath's distinguishing traits: utter disregard for the feelings of others, lying without remorse, difficulty in sustaining relationships, promiscuity, and endless manipulation to achieve their goals—meaning alcohol or drugs. Anyone in the throes of addiction definitely behaves like a sociopath in many ways.

In my case, it's easy to see why I blamed cocaine for all my misery. Everything had been great until Joe got addicted. Fortunately, there is help available for addicts. It is a manageable and treatable condition. After Joey cleaned up, we enjoyed what I thought were several absolutely charmed years, almost like a second honeymoon—which ended abruptly when Amy Fisher shot me in the head. Completely sober, and without drugs as an excuse for his inexcusable behavior, the truly sociopathic tendencies in my husband were starting to become more apparent. And for that, there is no cure.

CHAPTER 5

THE NARCISSIST
NEXT DOOR

I had to pat myself on the back: the move to the new house turned out to be a brilliant idea and made our having to go to my father-in-law for the down payment with our tails between our legs totally worthwhile. Our family was immediately absorbed into the warm, friendly community and its busy social life. Within weeks of the move, it felt like we'd been living there our whole lives. In a sense, Joey and I had: Massapequa was where we'd both grown up. Our kids would go to the same schools we had attended twenty-five years earlier. We had literally come home, and it felt good.

Clean and sober, Joe soon became hands-down the most popular guy on our block. He was a thoughtful and caring friend and neighbor. Nothing was too much trouble or too much to ask: Joey Buttafuoco would do anything for anybody, always with a joke and a smile. The phone rang often at all hours with panicky calls from people who were shaken up by a car accident or fender bender. Joey would immediately drive out to the scene, tow the car to Complete Auto Body, make sure they got home safely, and find them a replacement car to drive, reassuring them the whole time not to worry, it wasn't a big deal, and that he'd take care of everything, including the insurance hassles. And he did.

The neighborhood kids loved Joey, probably because he was just a big overgrown kid himself. He would patiently and endlessly play and clown around with Paul and Jessie and all their friends. He was unfailingly polite and respectful to all the other wives. After we settled into our productive, wonderful life in Massapequa, we were happy as honeymooners again. Grandparents and babysitters were minutes away. We took exotic anniversary getaway trips each year and had plenty of "couple time."

Joey was committed to sobriety and hard at work in the family business. I was busy with running the house—I was constantly decorating and improving it—board meetings of the beach club, various neighborhood committees, volunteer work, and most important, two growing kids and their numerous sports and social activities. I'd worked hard to save my marriage and was convinced—once we fully settled into our beautiful home, regained some financial stability, and saw our children thriving—that the long, hard struggle had been well worth it. I was happy, really happy to wake up each day and get moving. My panic attacks were a distant memory. Therapy had given me the tools to calm myself whenever I even started to feel anxious, which was rare. Life was good again.

While I imagined that this was the start of the rest of our lives, the sociopath I lived with thought that life was getting just a little bit too boring. I was thrilled with our ordinary existence: a spouse with a nine-to-five job, family dinners, paying the bills, watching a little TV or visiting friends at night, then going to bed and starting the same old routine all over again the next day. Living with a cocaine addict had been more than enough excitement for me.

Joey took up working out at the gym, and he became pretty obsessed with lifting weights, but I didn't give it a second thought. I assumed that after years of hard living, he was just generally becoming healthier. I worked out, too, and I was pleased that he was taking good care of himself. A more obvious sign of his restlessness and need for excitement was the boat. I always paid all the household bills, and one of the regular monthly expenses was our boat loan. We owned a nice twenty-four-foot boat with a small cuddy cabin that we docked at the marina next door every summer and put in dry dock in Freeport every winter. We enjoyed pulling the kids around behind us on inner tubes and taking friends out on the weekends for some water-skiing. I loved that boat; it provided us all with lots of good family fun.

One day in November 1990, Joey came to me and said, "Can I see the coupon book for the boat loan?"

"Sure, why?"

"Just want to take a look at it . . . I'm thinking about refinancing it and getting a better interest rate . . ." He was very vague.

It was no big deal. I handed him the coupon book and for-got all about it. I realized a month or two later that I hadn't seen the bill and reminded Joey that the boat loan was due. "Oh, don't worry about it. I've already taken care of it," he said.

"What exactly is going on—what are you doing?" I asked him.

"Nothing, nothing . . . geez, don't worry about it!" Joey said. Something was up, but as usual, no matter how much I questioned him, he always had an answer. Whatever. I had a house-hold to run and a million errands to do, so out of my head it went.

Three months later, I was taken to see the thirty-one-foot cigarette boat *Double Trouble* at a dealership close to our house. It was huge, with double engines, deafeningly loud, ostentatious, and completely over the top in every way. The inside was outfitted like the inside of a limousine, and twinkly lights were strung all over it. It was better equipped and plusher than many houses. I stood in the dealership where he had already bought this monstrosity—all the salesmen were congratulating me on our wise purchase—and could not believe it. This new toy cost $60,000.

Joey was grinning ear to ear. "Isn't this great?" he enthused. The look on my face made it clear that "great" was not my feel-ing. He knew full well what I was going to say when I started to speak and rushed to head me off. "Don't worry about it, don't worry about it . . . this is going to be so much fun. You and the kids are going to have a ball!"

I was furious. He took out a $60,000 loan without even discussing it with me? So *that's* what the evasive answers about the coupon book three months earlier had been about. He traded in our perfectly wonderful, perfectly adequate family boat and added sixty grand to our debt without even discussing the matter with me first! But, the deal was done; there was nothing to do but throw my hands up.

I was all alone in this fight; every one of my friends, not to mention their husbands, thought the racing boat was a fantastic idea. I was the wet blanket, fussing about how much it cost, how fast it went, and how somebody could easily get hurt. Meanwhile, all our friends and neighbors couldn't wait for summer to arrive so they could get out there and play. The kids and I didn't need this. But, hey, whatever. I put a smile on my face and went along for the ride, as usual.

When summer rolled around, I was soon forced to admit that the boat really was a lot of fun. The neighbors had an absolute ball. Our new toy was the biggest attraction at the beach club. Joey was like the Pied Piper, with people literally lining up for their turn to ride way out into the ocean and jump the waves. Our neighbor, a firefighter, spent a lot of time at the club with his younger brother, who had been paralyzed in a car accident and was wheelchair-bound. His accident was a real tragedy. He was a very nice guy and young, only in his late twenties. One day, Joey picked him up, carried him onto the boat, and took him out for a long ride. He was exhilarated and talked about it for weeks. He hadn't had that much fun in years. That was the kind of guy Joey was. By the end of August, even I had pretty much come around. The deceit and guise under which the boat was purchased faded from my memory.

The fall and winter of 1991 were peaceful and normal, at least as far as I knew. On the last night of the year, Joe and I attended a festive New Year's Eve party at the beach club. Surrounded by all our friends and neighbors, we made a champagne toast and kissed at midnight. "Ninety-one was great; ninety-two will be even better!" I had every reason to believe this was true.

With springtime came the annual round of confirmation parties and communion celebrations, which we "good" Catholics always attended. Some friends threw a lavish communion party for their seven-year-old daughter; they really pulled out all the stops. They rented a huge party boat for the official kickoff event of the summer, to be held on May 17. Everyone in the neighborhood looked forward to it for weeks. My thirty-seventh birthday was on Friday, May 15, and Joe and I had a low-key celebration, just out to dinner with some friends. That Sunday, the weather was perfect. Joe, the kids, and I got all dressed up, and as we walked onto the boat, a band serenaded us. The DJ got everybody up and dancing as we cruised Long Island Sound and had a delicious meal and drink. It was quite a bash.

Our next-door neighbors of six years had been transferred to Florida, and they were moving soon. I was in charge of collecting contributions from all the neighbors for a going-away gift. My friend Marilyn caught up to me for a minute at the party and said, "When do you want to go buy that gift? Tuesday or Wednesday?"

"The weather's going to be so nice this week . . . I'd really like to get that bench painted. . . . How about Wednesday?" I suggested.

On Monday, the day after the party, a flurry of people stopped by the house to drop off their money for the going-away gift. I put all the money, about $500 cash, in an envelope and stored it safely in my desk so I'd be ready for the shopping trip on Wednesday. (Needless to say, our neighbors never got their going-away gift.)

The next morning, Tuesday, I was allowing Paul and Jessica to ride their bikes to school with the neighborhood kids instead of taking the bus. The weather was beautiful, the end of the school year was approaching, and I didn't want to be overprotective. At nine and twelve they were old enough to ride along with their friends. I walked them out of the house, gave them each a kiss, and waved good-bye. Back inside, I finished the dishes, changed into some old clothes, gathered paint, gloves, and everything else I'd need for my project, went into the sunny backyard, and painted my bench . . . for about twenty minutes.

CHAPTER 6

NOTORIOUS J.O.E.

O ur tight-knit community threw a victory party in October 1992 when it was officially announced that, after a thorough investigation into the entire matter, no charges of any sort would be filed against Joey. The small celebration at the senior Buttafuoco's home turned into a huge raucous party as dozens of family members and friends stopped by to offer their support and good wishes. I was giddy with relief, vindication, and joy. Amy Fisher's official sentencing date was only weeks away. Once we got that behind us, maybe we could move on for good.

The outcome of the hearing was preordained. Due to her plea bargain, Amy would be sentenced to somewhere between five and fifteen years. No trial, but I would have my chance to speak up when I made a victim's impact statement in court. As the day approached, I grew more and more nervous. Every news organization in the world—no exaggeration—would be gathered at that courthouse. Television programming all over the country was preempted as every station went live to the courthouse on Long Island.

My parents, sister, and Cass and Bobby picked me up early on the morning of December 1 and drove me to the courthouse. Joey stayed home, as his presence would have been too distracting. This was my opportunity to speak out about how Amy's crime had affected me. For once, the attention would be focused on me, not the Joey and Amy sideshow. I had gained back a few pounds, my hair had grown out somewhat, and my balance was returning, but I was still in constant pain from continual ear infections. Nerves overtook me on the short ride over—three Valium, and I was still shaking like a leaf. I knew the speech I would make in that courtroom would be seen by the whole world. Not to mention that this was the first time I'd see Amy since that day on the porch.

Our arrival was greeted by the most incredible mob scene, with the police fighting to hold back the press and shouting, "Make room, make way!" Flashbulbs were popping, lights were in our faces, everyone was pushing and shoving, and reporters shouted questions. We put our heads down and inched into the courtroom, fighting every step of the way.

The packed courtroom, once we got seated, was a welcome respite. After I took my seat and got my bearings, I got a good look at Amy's parents and gave them the dirtiest look I could. *What did you do to that kid? One child, and this is the best you could do?* were my uncharitable thoughts at the time. Anger stiffened my resolve, overshadowed my fear, and got me to my feet to make my speech when I was called.

"I was left for dead with a .25 caliber bullet lodged in my head, one inch from my spinal cord. As a result of this vicious and violent act, my life and the lives of my family have changed completely . . ." My voice grew stronger as I recounted what had happened to me, detailed my injuries, and finally took the chance to tell Amy, directly to her face, that what shocked me most was her nonchalant attitude and utter lack of remorse.

The judge had some harsh words for Amy. "In the eyes of this court you are a tragedy and a disgrace—to yourself, to your friends, family, and to society. You deserve no less than the maximum sentence I can impose by law—a minimum of five years with a maximum of fifteen years." The gavel banged, and all of the legal proceedings were finally over—or so I thought.

Then, as if my day hadn't been surreal enough, I went home and packed for my trip to Hollywood. The race for a television movie of the week was on. All three networks were currently shooting their own movie about the case. One was Amy's version, one was a journalist's version, and the CBS movie was told from our—mine and Joey's—point of view. Amy had been paid a ton of money for book and movie rights, so I had no qualms about accepting money for the rights to make our story into a TV movie. The other movies would be made with or without my permission. Everyone, but most especially the perpetrator, was cashing in on this story. We had hundreds of thousands of dollars' worth of legal and medical bills, not to mention an elaborate new security system. The movie money—and any paid appearances on television shows—was blood money, for sure, but it had been my blood. I was willing to take it.

A trip to Hollywood and a visit to a movie set where our story was being filmed should have been a fun and exciting adventure. *Casualty of Love* starred Jack Scalia and Alyssa Milano, and after we landed in L.A., we were driven to a fancy Beverly Hills hotel. The next day, a limousine drove us to a distant L.A. neighborhood where the film was shooting on location, and we met the actors and observed. I felt queasy all day. The stress of Amy's sentencing and the long plane ride had been too much for me. That night in our beautiful hotel room, a vicious headache—different from the regular pain I lived with—blindsided me. I couldn't stop vomiting and quickly became dehydrated. I wound up in Cedars-Sinai Medical Center for the next two days. My symptoms were so severe that the doctors feared I had meningitis. Shopping and sightseeing in the sun were forgotten. I was forced to return home early to consult my regular doctors.

I made it home and eventually recovered. All three TV movies aired on the same weekend. The worst year of my life came to a close. The whole case and its attendant publicity should have been over and done with. But with Amy securely behind prison bars, public opinion once again swayed. Now there was a strong, lingering feeling among the general public that Joe had gotten away with something. Given the inflammatory press headlines about him, I could see why. He had been portrayed as a rapist, a conspirator to murder his wife, the worst kind of cheater and liar in the headlines for months.

The outcry had risen to such a fever pitch that Michael Rindenow advised us to retain a criminal attorney, just in case. Marvyn Kornberg, a prominent attorney best known for representing cops in trouble, entered our lives. He and Joey became very close.

The official announcement that Joey had been cleared did nothing to stop the coverage. Matters got to the point where Geraldo Rivera actually held a mock trial on his show, playacting what the charges would have been if Joey had been indicted, complete with a judge and jury. Legal experts were all over the airwaves slamming Joey, insisting that he had had everything to do with this girl's actions. We saw it differently, of course. The story was over, but it had been such a ratings bonanza for months that the media was going to find every angle they could to keep this story going.

This crucifixion by media was very upsetting to all our families and it wasn't going away. Marvyn convinced all of us that we needed to take the offensive. This meant a media blitz to clear Joe's name. Joe was all for it. He liked the press; he had become friendly with many of the reporters covering the story. He actually used to bring pizza to the reporters camped out on our lawn! They enjoyed talking and kidding around together. It didn't escape my notice that Joe thrived on the attention and had especially loved being on a movie set in L.A.

"Enough, Joe," I told him wearily, several times. "It's over. Let's try to get back to a normal life."

"Oh, no, Mary Jo—I need to clear my name!" Getting his

good name back became a huge mission for him, and he soon became obsessed with the idea. Now, let's think for a moment how a normal person in this situation would behave. He was getting away with no legal repercussions, not to mention that he had the full support of both our families and an entire neighborhood full of people standing firmly behind him. His wife was alive and functioning, and our friends and neighbors went out of their way to insulate us from the harshness that awaited us outside of our community.

Wouldn't a normal person say to himself, "Whew, I dodged a bullet on that one," *shut up*, and put the incident behind him, no matter what the press said? Maybe think about devoting the rest of his life to being a good partner to his badly injured spouse? That's what I would have done; I think that's what most people would do in such a situation. But fame—or notoriety might be a better term—had come to us, a very unwanted and unwelcome development for me, but not for Joey. Whenever he started in about his mission to clear his name, all I could rationalize was, *Huh! He* must *be innocent, or he'd let this thing die. He really does want to vindicate himself like any normal, innocent person who gets falsely accused of something.*

I agreed to join him for an appearance on *The Phil Donahue Show* in this misguided campaign in January 1993, less than eight months after I'd been shot. I was in no shape to make a public appearance anywhere, but I had made the commitment and felt I should honor it. I was mainly there to support Joey. I knew he was very far from the monster the press continued to portray. I liked *The Phil Donahue Show* and had watched it for years. From what I'd seen, Phil seemed like a warm, engaging man who really listened and was polite and respectful to his guests.

Both sets of parents, several family members, and a few neighbors showed up to sit in the audience at the show, where the other audience members proceeded to vilify Joe and attack me, too. "Yes, I knew her. Yes, I drove her home, but I never did anything . . ." was the gist of what he said over and over. The audience wasn't buying it. All the viewers felt very free to berate me for what they saw as my stupidity as I sat there frozen like a deer in the headlights. This audience whipped themselves into an absolute finger-pointing, name-calling frenzy. It was horrible. I felt as close as I could to being trapped on an episode of *The Jerry Springer Show*. What happened while we were sitting on that stage was the furthest thing imaginable from the calm, reasonable, back-and-forth discussion I had envisioned.

On the way home from what had been a trying ordeal, I said, "I'm done. Joey. I *am done* with all this. No traveling, no appearances anywhere. I just want to concentrate on getting better." I was such an easy target for the press. My paralyzed face, garbled speech, and devotion to Joey had been mocked endlessly nationwide on *Saturday Night Live,* newspapers, television shows, and radio. Not only did this hurt my feelings terribly, but it made me angrier. We were out of our league when it came to the media, and I had the sense to realize it.

That was it for me, but Joe and Kornberg continued on the

great Joey Buttafuoco "I'm Clearing My Name Tour." The whole idea was absurd. He wasn't facing any charges; therefore my husband had no need for a lawyer. But Kornberg loved seeing his own face on television and wanted to extend his fifteen minutes. There was no good reason for Joey to be anywhere talking about anything; the whole episode was over and done with. But he and his lawyer egged each other on. Some of these appearances were paid, which I had no problem with—*that* I could at least understand. What I did have a problem with was how much he loved the publicity. Joey and Marvyn were a terrible match, and the harm he did Joey was incalculable.

When Larry King called, they were both quite anxious to appear. Both did their best to convince me to join them, but I absolutely refused. So, Dumb and Dumber showed up on *Larry King Live* saying, "The cops messed this case up . . . they're stupid . . . they're morons . . ." and denigrating them at every turn. Larry, meanwhile, asked a question about the receipt Joey had supposedly signed at a local motel. "Well, what about this motel receipt? It looks like you signed it."

"Oh, that's not my handwriting!" Joey went on and on about how he'd been framed. It was clear that he believed he could talk anybody into anything. In fact, I believe he had talked *himself* into believing his own version of events. It had worked pretty well so far, anyway.

Joey's behavior was a textbook example of a very interesting phenomenon: the inability of many sociopaths to close their mouths and resist the spotlight, even when it's clear to the whole world that they should just lie low and *shut up*. O. J. Simpson and Scott Peterson, for example, would later display this same trait—rambling on and on in the misguided belief that their version of events made sense, with the absolute conviction that given the chance to talk long enough and explain it well enough, they could convince everyone of the "truth." But back then this was all uncharted territory. We had the dubious distinction of being the hottest "real people" crime story to catch America's imagination in years.

Joey simply could not stop talking—the downfall of a sociopath. The district attorney and cops back on Long Island, meanwhile, were far from pleased with this barrage of bad publicity. They were already being bombarded with angry phone calls and letters from people all over the country asking, "How could you let this child molester/rapist/murder plot participant *off*?" Meanwhile, there he was on TV every night, badmouthing these very same authorities. Prosecuting Joey hadn't been worth the DA's time. Because Amy's crime had been so egregious and her behavior so callous, they really didn't want to bother going after Joe once they realized she had acted alone. That feeling sure changed after a few nationwide appearances from Joe and his lawyer. Behind the scenes, a grand jury convened to investigate Amy's allegations of statutory rape. The authorities started pulling together an indictment.

In April 1993—ten months after I was shot and five months after the decision that Joey would not be charged in connection with the crime—the DA's office announced to the press that they were going after Joey: sixteen counts of statutory rape, twelve counts of third-degree sodomy, and one count of endangering the welfare of a child. Each count was a felony carrying a possible penalty of one to four years. He could conceivably be put away for more than ninety years—a situation I blamed entirely on the fact that he and his lawyer could not manage to close their mouths. The two of them, and their big mouths, and their spotlight. This is what had come of the great campaign.

I literally lost my mind when Marvyn called to break the news. I started screaming like a banshee, never mind that the children were in the house and my outburst was scaring them to death. No matter what, I had kept up a strong front for Paul and Jessie. I refused to let my behavior traumatize them further. I had told them a hundred ways and a million times that I was going to be all right. Not this time. I completely lost control. Joe raced into the room and tried to put his arms around me to calm me. I flailed away at him in a white-hot rage, wailing and cursing at the top of my lungs. I was making so much noise that our next-door neighbors could hear me and came running over. I screamed at them, too, and pushed them away when they tried to approach. Eventually, I fell to the floor, pounding and kicking and screaming even louder.

Everyone was horrified. No one knew how to handle this situation. "Mommy, you're the fighting Irish," nine-year-old Jessica pleaded, referring to a Notre Dame baseball cap I wore during my recovery. "You'll be okay."

"No!" I screamed at my wide-eyed, terrified daughter. "It's not okay. Nothing is ever going to be okay again! This nightmare will never end!" Joe eventually called the police. My fit showed no signs of ending, and no one knew what to do for me. The officers said they were on their way (we were on a first-name basis with every cop in town by then), and advised Joey to call my doctor.

The doctor, who could hear me yelling in the background over the phone, told Joe to find the strongest sedative he could in the jumble of all my prescription bottles. There were some pills there I had never even used. Joey forced me to swallow two of them. "Sure! Give them all to me! I want to take them all and die! I can't go on like this!" I screamed.

When the police entered the house, I immediately turned my rage onto them.

"This is all your fault, all of it! What the fuck is the matter with all of you? Some teenage hooker does her best to murder me, and this is what happens? Indicting my husband is how you all help me? Assholes!" My tirade lasted at least ten more minutes until I had completely worn myself out. At that point, of course, Joe had to comfort me, literally carry me to bed, and try to reassure me that everything would be all right. "You and that fucking lawyer of yours—he ought to go to jail with you!" I told him before passing out.

Our spring and summer were spent in legal limbo as we tried to figure out the best thing to do about this vengeful DA. The situation bordered on the absurd; the sheer number of separate counts was completely over the top. The authorities were really gunning for him. We truly believed Joey was being obviously and unfairly persecuted.

In the end, at the bargaining table, Joe agreed to plead guilty to one count of statutory rape and was sentenced to six months in county jail, a $5,000 fine, and five years' probation. Joe painted this plea bargain as a sacrifice he was making to end all this madness. He was completely innocent, he swore, but plenty of innocent people rot in jail for things they didn't do. He was the victim of overzealous prosecutors. I agreed with him completely on that point, but I didn't bother to point out that he had brought this whole mess on himself.

The media circus was back on. Once again, the eyes of the world were fixed squarely on the Massapequa courthouse on the day Joe formally went before the judge and entered his plea. "On July 2, 1991, I had sexual relations with Amy Fisher at the Freeport Motel," Joey said in court, sealing his image as a cheating, lying scumbag forever in the mind of the public.

Amy was let out of Albion Correctional Facility near Buffalo, where she was serving her time, to attend his hearing and make her own victim's impact statement. Her hair was in ringlets, and she wore a demure dress with kneesocks like a little girl. And who was standing right by her side? Assistant District Attorney Klein—the same man who stood next to me when I, as the victim of attempted murder with a bullet still lodged in my head, made my statement at her trial—the man who had repeatedly referred to Amy as a "wild animal" and "not credible" in the press. I took it as a personal slap to my face.

Amy made quite a speech about Joe introducing her, a regular sixteen-year-old girl, to expensive restaurants and cheap motels. She didn't look up once. She was clearly reading what someone had written for her. It was all utter crap. Her appearance and words absolutely enraged me as I watched her live on TV. There was nothing that could have induced me to accompany Joey to court that day. I refused to be present and compelled to lay eyes on her again. When this entire farce was over, I fired Marvyn Kornberg immediately. He had done nothing but harm.

In November 1993, Joe went off to serve his time in the local jail. My anger, never far from the surface, reached a fever pitch when I contemplated a winter on my own. Our house had become a target. Rarely did a day pass without a carload of gawkers who posed for pictures on the lawn, drove by and yelled insults, or, in many cases, threw eggs or trash at the house. Carloads of teenagers raced by at night, whooping and yelling. I was afraid to be alone at home with the kids all winter. It was certainly no secret to anyone in America where we lived. We had installed a massive security system with cameras and alarms, but that didn't stop the circus outside on the street.

"What are you going to do if something happens to me?" I demanded of the police. "I'm already harassed daily when Joe is home. Now I'll be all alone with two children, and I'm not in the best of shape!" My ear continued to give me trouble with constant infections, and the pain was ever-present. Imagine the worst toothache and migraine you've ever had—combined—all the time. I was taking heavy doses of painkillers, which rendered me pretty much a functioning vegetable. I was incapable of protecting myself should that need arise. Their solution was to park an empty Nassau County police car directly in front of our house as a deterrent to mischief-makers.

Record-breaking freezing temperatures and snowfall descended on Long Island that year, making for an endless, miserable winter. I did my best to celebrate Thanksgiving and Christmas for the kids, who missed their father badly. Joe was allowed three visits per week, and I tried to go as often as possible. Going to visit my husband in jail was a degrading, dehumanizing process. All the visitors stood in line outside for a couple of hours in the bitter cold and dirty, mushy snow, waiting to be processed for as long as it took. Inside, the officers took everything from me, even the rubber band holding my hair in a ponytail, so I soon learned to show up empty-handed. The staff at the jail couldn't have cared less that I was Mary Jo Buttafuoco, the notorious woman they saw every single night on TV, or that my physical condition was still fragile. There was no special treatment for me, so I endured the finger-pointing, whispering, and downright rude questions and comments from all the other visitors every single time.

Not surprisingly, Joe did quite well in jail. He was housed in a special wing for high-profile cases, and he soon charmed the guards as he did everyone else. They even brought him special meals on the holidays. He was doing fine. Meanwhile, I was an absolute wreck at home. I was thrilled when he was released early in March for good behavior, and so was everybody else. If I thought I'd seen a party before, that was nothing compared to this.

Friends and lawyers insisted on throwing a huge, black-tie, invitation-only homecoming party at a restaurant the week Joe got released. I was ambivalent. I was simply relieved to have him back home to help me. I certainly didn't need a party. My friends, however, made all the arrangements. They wanted some sort of official celebration, so I allowed them to talk me into it. One friend sent out invitations, another booked limousines, and a good friend of the family offered to host the party at his popular local restaurant Testarossa. The press turned out to cover his homecoming, the neighbors arrived in full force to show their support, and the night was one long, joyful gala. Jessica refused to leave her father's side all night. In every single picture of Joe taken that night, our ten-year-old daughter was right there next to him, glued to his side, almost as if she was afraid to let him out of her sight.

At the time, I believed that nothing worse than what I'd already endured could ever conceivably happen. Amy was safely locked up in prison, and while Joe had foolishly talked himself into jail, he was safe, out, and back home with us. Spring had finally arrived after the worst winter I could ever remember. We were going to put all this behind us once and for all now. I was sure of it.

CHAPTER 7

GOOD-BYE L.I., HELLO L.A.

There was only one thing I wanted out of life: a return to a normal existence. I had been fighting to recover from my devastating injury with everything I had for two years. I was determined to be present for my kids, which sustained me through three separate operations. The first, which I jokingly referred to as my half-assed facelift, corrected the drooping skin hanging from the paralyzed side of my face. It definitely improved my appearance, but my face was still lopsided and would remain so forever. Much worse than how I looked were the ongoing inner ear infections. My injured ear canal continually oozed and dripped. When an infection was really raging, the pain became nearly unbearable. Doctors did their best to fix the damage deep inside my skull in two separate operations, but after the second operation, we all conceded that I would have to simply learn to live with recurring ear problems.

Sheer anger and determination had kept me going through the longest, darkest winter of my life. I'd enjoyed six charmed years in my beautiful home, and I meant to get back to that life, whatever it took. My ever-present rage—at Amy, the authorities who should have looked out for me as a crime victim, the loss of my anonymity, the irreparable damage done to my family—was now tempered by a feeling of overwhelming gratitude that the nightmare I'd been living might actually be over.

Joe and I made several trips to Los Angeles over the next year. Los Angeles was a place I enjoyed visiting. These trips meant a stay in a lovely hotel, sightseeing, and a quick appearance by Joe on a talk show. Amazingly enough, the media still wanted to rehash the story, and now Joe had a new angle: how he'd made a deal and served time in jail to ease the pain and suffering of his family and put an end to the nightmare. He, too, was a victim of Amy Fisher. Some of these appearances were paid, but this was Joe's favorite topic—he was happy to expound on it for free. I looked at these jaunts as mini-vacations, though I would have preferred to never speak of any of these events ever again. But Joe continued to fan the flames. Without his constant presence on TV, the whole sordid story would have eventually died a natural death. Sure, it would have always been an interesting bit of news, a point of interest, but nothing like it was. But despite a term in jail, Joe refused to let it go!

A female talent agent approached Joe and told him, "I think we can parlay your name recognition into an entertainment career." This woman, Sherri Spillane, was very credible. She and her partner Ruth Webb handled many of the old Hollywood stars like Mickey Rooney, and I liked her very much. She and her partner were just entering the reality field, a very novel idea back then. We were real, all right.

I was the wet blanket, as usual. I thought the whole idea was stupid. Once again, I felt lost in the shuffle. I had almost been murdered. Was that something to base an entertainment career on? I kept waiting and hoping for the day that Joey would say something like, "Are you crazy? My wife was almost killed in cold blood in front of her own house. I would never capitalize on that or try to parlay it into anything!" I waited in vain because he never said anything of the kind. The spotlight was just too intoxicating. He loved the idea of having an agent. "They're doing this to us, Mary Jo," was again his reasoning. "We haven't caused this, but it all happened. We can't change any of it, so we might as well make money from it!" I didn't agree, but if it meant a few trips to the West Coast each year, then fine.

I had recovered enough to go about my regular life again—errands, carpooling, housework—and Joe was back at work, where life had finally returned to business as usual. Oh, Complete Auto Body got the occasional prank call or curious tourist, but for the most part they were going about the business of auto body repair again in blissful anonymity. Joey and I were in great shape financially—we'd received settlements from both Amy Fisher's and Peter Guagenti's parents' homeowners' policies, plus the Hollywood TV movie money.

Three years after the shooting, the window to a regular, normal life had cracked open. I had the feeling, not that I dared to put it into words, but for the first time I felt deep inside, *Maybe we are going to make it. Everything's finally going to be all right.* The only cloud on the horizon was the health of my father-in-law. Cass, a nonsmoker all his life, was diagnosed with lung cancer. His doctors theorized that it was caused by working around asbestos on submarines during his service in World War II. Mesothelioma was a terrible disease, and it quickly weakened my vital, powerful father-in-law into a shadow of his former self. That, and the regular visits from Joe's parole officer, who interviewed me periodically at our house, still fueled my rage. I was still very angry at the system. I hated being forced to answer their standard questions about whether or not Joe was doing drugs, hitting me, had a job—more unnecessary harassment, as far as I was concerned.

Cass's doctors did their best to alleviate his pain, and he went through a number of unofficial drug trials as they searched for the right combination. Industrial-size pill bottles were all over his bedroom, including a container that held 120 Percocet. Cass took two, but they didn't agree with him at all, and the doctors moved on to other drugs. I, meanwhile, kept a covetous eye on that huge bottle of pills. I had my own standing prescription for Percocet, but my doctors were giving me an increasingly hard time about my frequent refills. They kept telling me I was taking too much; I kept telling them I was in pain. When several days passed and no one touched Cass's discarded bottle, I scooped it into my purse one afternoon. I should have been ashamed to steal medicine from my terminally ill father-in-law, whether or not he intended to take it, but I was elated at the prospect of 118 extra pills I wouldn't have to fight to get.

In May 1995, Joey flew out to L.A. for an art show. Usually, I accompanied him on these trips. This time, however, I wanted to attend end-of-the-school-year meetings for the kids and a friend's birthday lunch, so Joey went by himself. He was the L.A. attraction, anyway—not me. The night after he left, I was jolted out of a sound sleep in the middle of the night by a phone call from our new attorney, Dominic Barbara.

"Joey's been arrested in Hollywood," he said.

"What? For what . . . what are you talking about?" I said, still half-asleep.

"For soliciting a hooker," Dominic said. He assured me that he was taking care of the matter. He would handle the legalities over the phone with Joe's court-appointed lawyer first thing the next morning. He had called in the middle of the night to warn me because the arrest would hit the newswire any minute. And make no mistake about it, this would be big news.

Right there, at that moment, in my dark bedroom in the middle of the night, sitting all alone listening to the voice on the other end of the phone line, something inside of me died: a vital force that hadn't been destroyed by the shooting, the trials, or by Joe going to jail. I had stayed strong throughout all that, my inner core fired by anger more than anything—it had been a great motivator. This was different. I wilted like a broken flower. I literally fell out of bed onto the floor and curled up into a ball.

Joey had served time for statutory rape. He swore up and

down that he didn't do it, and we all believed him. But to now get arrested for soliciting a hooker? It just had to be something sex-related, didn't it? I saw myself sliding right back down into a cesspool after three years of everybody standing by my husband, trusting in his word and innocence, really believing he took that plea not because he'd done anything wrong, but because he was so railroaded that there was no other choice. This was how my family, our friends, all the wonderful people who'd stood by us would be paid back for our love and loyalty?

I couldn't contain my anger and disappointment when Joey was eventually allowed to make a call home. What a surprise: *it wasn't his fault.* He had a reasonable explanation and plenty of excuses, as usual. He had just been sitting in his car in a parking lot outside a convenience store in Hollywood, minding his own business, according to him. "I'm getting on a plane right now. I'll be home tonight and explain everything . . . but I didn't do anything!"

I slammed the phone down. It immediately rang again.

It was Howard Stern, live and on the air at 6:00 AM, already on top of the latest Buttafuoco scandal. He sure caught me at the wrong moment—I didn't hold back. "That asshole! I can't believe he did this!" I screamed to America over the airwaves. His whole crew was laughing, joking, egging me on. It was great entertainment for them and their audience, I'm sure. Fortunately, Paul and Jessie slept through the call and my tirade. When I hung up the phone, it hit me. I've got to call my parents and tell them. And Joe's family—and his father is dying!

Of course, I still had to get the kids up and out the door to school and pretend everything was all right, that it was just another day, which I managed somehow. The three of us got ready for school, ate breakfast, and started the day. I didn't say a word about the phone call, or that their father had been busted again, or anything else. Once they were safely on their way, I called a close friend, broke the news, and arranged for her to keep the kids overnight. Then I fell apart.

By the time Joe came home that night, the press was back in full force—camped out in the yard and in the street, with lights, cameras, and news crews. It was déjà vu in the worst way. I had never spoken to Joe like I did that night—because the kids were at my friend's house. My words were bitter and terrible, and my behavior nothing I'm proud of. I called him every name in the book. It was no way for husbands or wives to ever speak to each other, but I had been driven beyond my level of tolerance. We had descended into madness.

His story was that a hooker had been leaning up against the outside wall of a convenience store where he had stopped. "Some woman came up to the car, and I rolled down the window. She asked me if I wanted company. I was just joking around and said, 'You look like you're worth about thirty dollars!' We laughed, I drove away, and next thing I know a bunch of police cars surround me and arrest me for soliciting! She was an undercover cop! I didn't do anything; I didn't even leave the car!"

"Why did you roll down that window? Why say anything at

all? Why can't you ever shut the fuck up?! When are you going to understand that we are not normal people anymore? That we're targets?" But I was wasting my breath.

At one point that night, I could not endure it any longer. I stood up right in the middle of something Joey was saying, left him and a couple of family members sitting in the living room, climbed the stairs, entered my bathroom, and looked at all the pills in my medicine cabinet. There were plenty of them. I held all the bottles in my hand and seriously contemplated swallowing every last pill in every last container. I literally did not want to be in this nightmare anymore. I knew I couldn't live through it again. There is no doubt I would have checked out then and there—I truly wanted to die—but I couldn't leave my children alone during this mess. So I swallowed a double dose of Xanax, crawled into my bed, and pulled the covers over my head.

I was done, I was tired, I wasn't moving, and I didn't care who said what to me. Keeping up appearances was over. All the strength, anger, and resolve that had kept me going for the past three years disappeared, leaving only an empty shell. Forget getting the kids ready for school, driving them places, greeting them when they arrived home in the afternoons, games, schedules, homework, meetings. "You deal with it," I told my husband. "You figure it out because I am done. Oh, and find somewhere else to sleep. This room is taken." The kids came into my room to visit me after school the next day, and when they started telling me what they needed that day, that night, and for school, I just looked at Joe and said, "Figure it out because I am done. Mommy doesn't feel well." I rolled over and dived under the covers again.

This was a really alarming development for Joe. I dropped the ball in a big way— I let it all go. After a few days of me refusing to get up, Joe frantically called my closest girlfriends. "You've got to come over and talk to her. I've never seen her like this." When they showed up to check on me, and gently and reasonably pointed out, "You can't just lay here like this forever," I replied, "I don't give a shit! The house can burn down for all I care. I'm staying right here." I wasn't going to kill myself, but it sure would have been nice to go to sleep and not wake up.

The will to live is actually much stronger than I had ever realized. Eventually, of course, I wanted to clean up. I got hungry. I had to get out of bed, shower, go downstairs, fix something to eat, and resume living—if for no other reason than Cass really was dying. Joe's help was desperately needed at the shop, and the family needed me at their home. Cass was aware of Joey's latest "situation," but he was so heavily medicated that I'm not sure how much he really understood, which was a blessing. My parents, on the other hand, were very much alive and well. And they were pissed!

My father, the most mild-mannered, polite, pleasant banker type you could ever hope to meet, insisted on a family meeting at the senior Buttafuocos' home. Cass was too weak to even make it downstairs on the appointed night, but my parents and

Joe's sisters, stepmother, brother Bobby, and Joe and I all sat in the living room as my quiet, reserved father tore into Joe. "What are you doing to my daughter and the children? Just what do you think you're doing to this family? Your actions affect all of us!"

Joe continued to protest that he was set up, he hadn't done anything wrong, and on and on, but my father, for one, wasn't listening. Disillusionment had set in for my parents, and they saw the writing on the wall. Joe was remorseful and just sat there, taking my father's tongue-lashing.

I was stuck. I was up and out of bed, but my spirit was gone. Depression robbed me of the energy it would have taken to pack up and leave Joe. The timing was also dreadful. I loved my father-in-law dearly. I wanted to help however I could, to be at his side during his final days and help my family in their time of need. There were bigger problems going on than Joey's sideshow; this was literally life and death. I was forced to put my own troubles aside. All my time was taken up with the death vigil. It wasn't just the family repercussions we had to deal with—it was a legal quagmire. Joe had been on probation at the time of his hooker scandal, and I knew the repercussions would be severe. I was the only one worried about it. Joe was his typical, breezy self about the matter. "What—are you kidding? They're not going to put me in jail over this!"

"They certainly are!" Here we went again. Sociopaths are simply not frightened by the things others are. That grandiose sense of self does not allow for fear. Rules and regulations are for the rest of the world, not them. Mind you, Joe had already served time. Most people would do whatever it took to stay the hell out of the penal system for the rest of their lives. With typical insouciance, Joe wasn't worried. That was my job. And sure enough, in June he was officially sentenced to jail for three months, to be served starting in September.

Cass died in August, and very soon afterward Joe went back to jail. It was a blessing that his father didn't live to see that, and a mercy that he was only fuzzily aware of the entire drama playing out during the last few months of his life. Joe was gone, and I made up my mind. For real, I was leaving. I did not visit Joe one time during those seventy-five days. Nor did I miss him—not one little bit.

I refused all his phone calls, though I allowed the kids to take them. Paul was now fifteen, and he refused to even discuss his father's current difficulty with me. Jessica was much more upset—by what she saw as the unfairness of it all. Joey had, of course, given the children his version of what had happened and had sworn it was a big misunderstanding, not his fault. She, for one, believed every word. She was 100 percent on his side. I did what I could: hugged them, told them how much I loved them, encouraged them to lean on their family and friends.

It was actually a very peaceful two and a half months in one sense. I was financially secure and knew exactly where my husband was and what he was doing. I had plenty of time to reflect on Joey's behavior, without his endless justifications and wheedling and joking. I came to the conclusion that there weren't going to be any more surprises in my life. I steeled myself to break the news to the kids.

I took Paul and Jessica out to dinner one night and said, "Kids, I have to talk to you about something important. When Dad gets out of jail, I am going to ask him for a separation. I am having a very hard time with all this, and I can't live like this anymore."

Twelve-year-old Jessica burst into tears. "You can't do that! Daddy needs us! How can you do this to him? He's in jail!" Paul didn't have a visible reaction one way or another, but Jessica was beside herself. She was Daddy's girl, for sure, and was really suffering because he was away.

"Mom, if you break up with Daddy, I'm going to go live with *him*!" she said. I tried to reach over and comfort her, but she wouldn't let me touch her. She was furious with me. I started to backpedal.

"All right, I wanted to bring this up tonight. It's something to think about," I said, and then we went home. Jessica absolutely refused to speak to me for the rest of the night and disappeared into her room with the slam of a door. I sat up late that night and realized that I was stuck. I was tired, I was hurt, and I didn't want to be in this marriage anymore. But my daughter was so hysterical, and Paul was so stoic. I couldn't do this to them.

When Joe returned home in December, he was chastened and sorry. Again, of course. "You can't leave me now. I need you more than ever! Dad is dead, and Bobby says I can't come back to the shop!"

Bobby had apparently gone to see Joe in jail and told him he was not welcome back at work because Joey was bad for business. More bad news—but the holidays were upon us, and we had to get through them somehow. Family tradition dictated that we celebrate Christmas at the Buttafuoco home, but we all needed a change of venue. It would have been too sad a reminder that Cass was gone to gather at Joey's childhood home just months after his death. I offered to host the family at our house that year. The situation was awkward, to say the least, but I filled the house with friends as well as family so we wouldn't have to interact too much. All of us were cordial. I was mortified inside, but put on a happy face. I gave gifts to Bobby's children gifts, of course, and chatted a bit with their parents.

According to Joe, Bobby's wife Ursula was behind this decision to oust him from the shop. She had put her foot down and told Bobby to make a choice: either his brother or his wife and kids. Joe was enraged; he blamed her completely for this breach. The family business was his birthright, and some outsider was taking it away! Joe, as usual, was quite convincing. And as he ranted endlessly about his treacherous sister-in-law, his anger began to spark mine. How *could* they do this to us— take away our livelihood just when we needed it most?

Bobby had laid it on the line: Complete Auto Body and Repair was sinking. No one wanted to bring their cars in for service there. The place had become a joke. All that was in the public's mind was, "Didn't some guy have sex with a teenage girl there?" Cass's legacy was going down the tubes, and there was only one reason. Bobby and his wife had young children to support. Bobby, like Joe, had worked there his whole life. Joe was no longer an owner; it was solely Bobby's business after Cass died. The decision was final: Joe was not allowed to work there anymore. After that Christmas, despite my understanding of the realities of what was happening with the business, I no longer spoke to Bobby or Ursula, whom I'd loved for many years.

Joey's frequent outbursts only added fuel to my fire. Whether or not it was in my mind, or it really happened, I felt people pulling away from us. There was a general sense of those around us backing away. *You know, Joey, I made an ass out of myself for years defending you. Then you're out in L.A. soliciting a hooker?* I was in a total state of depressed resignation. On top of that, I felt plenty of shame, fear, and embarrassment. The kids didn't want me to leave their father, and where was I going to go, anyway? I swallowed some more pills and soldiered on.

I lived for ten years in my dream house. Six of them happy. But it wasn't my dream house anymore. Friends and neighbors had distanced themselves—the second media onslaught had been a little too much for many of them. The family was fractured over Joe's firing from his own family business. Clearly, there was nothing left for my family on Long Island. We put the house on the market and hoped for the best. We weren't sure if its notoriety would make the house an easy sell or an impossible one.

Where do you go to live when you're infamous and hope just to blend in with the crowd? "I can work in L.A.!" Joe said. "We can start a whole new life there! It'll be great!" He had created this whole mess, but here was the solution. I had no desire to live in California. I lived exactly where I wanted to live. But even on days when I told myself it wasn't too late that I could still get out of this marriage, I knew I could never bring myself to let Joe go out to California alone and worry about the kids going back and forth to visit him if we separated. I was going where they were going; I had to stick it out. *They've been through so much,* was the constant refrain in my mind. It was all I could think of. They needed both their mother and their father.

And I needed my pills. Once we finally decided to make the move, *Where am I going to get my supply?* was one of my biggest concerns. I needed those Xanax and Percocet just to get through the day. By the time we left Long Island, I was taking twenty-seven pills every twenty-four hours.

Packing up that house broke my heart. On a hot summer day, the biggest moving van I'd ever seen in my life hauled away every single one of our possessions, along with three cars we had to transport across the country. The four of us stayed at my parents' house for three days to give the furniture truck time to arrive before we flew west. It was a sad, quiet time. My parents had visibly aged during the past few years. The whole matter had crushed them both. Less than a year later, they also packed up and moved north to rural Maine. My situation destroyed my father: first of all, the shock of almost losing his daughter, but then the whole out-of-control circus and public humiliation that followed. Massapequa was such a small community; everywhere he went there were comments about the case, remarks, pointed fingers. He'd be in the diner trying to have a cup of coffee and hear people making salacious remarks about Joe and Amy. It was suffocating; there was no getting away from it.

Despite all I'd been through in the past seven years, I had never even been tempted to pick up a cigarette, a habit I'd shed when the kids were small. The day before we moved to California, I drove to the convenience store, bought a couple of packs, and started puffing away. What the hell did smoking, or my health, matter? I no longer cared about anything anymore.

Our feeling was that we were living in la-la land, just another couple of loonies new on the scene. When everybody's pointing at you all the time, it's nice to live in a place where there are lots of others to point at, too. There weren't many famous people living on Long Island—and those who did lived on gated estates in Brookville or South Hampton and had servants shop for them. They weren't strolling through the local Pathmark grocery store twice a week, like I had.

Joe didn't have a job or any work lined up. We lived on the proceeds from the sale of our house—which sold after four months on the market—and waited to see what would develop. We rented a nice home in the San Fernando Valley, which we chose based on the reputation of the school system. Fortunately for me, Sherri, our new agent, recommended an accommodating general practitioner. When you have a bullet in the side of your head, doctors don't tend to say no. Whatever I wanted in terms of prescriptions was filled on the spot, no questions asked. "What do you need? How much of it?" were the only questions they ever asked at his office. My pill intake, already quite high, escalated.

Joey bounced around L.A., making plenty of friends wherever he went. Californians—many of whom were transplants themselves—were very mellow, nice, and accepting of our history. If anything, I think people were just surprised to see that we were a decent couple, not the freaks they'd read about in the tabloids. Joe found work as a bouncer at the Rainbow Room on Sunset Strip, a perfect job for the short term.

Jessica entered eighth grade, and Paul entered eleventh. Jessica, particularly, appeared to adjust fairly well and quickly, making new friends and playing sports. God bless my daughter . . . she has the good part of Joe's personality in her. She makes the best of situations, gets involved in activities, and has a very resilient spirit. Paul, meanwhile, is much more reserved and holds things in.

Paul was essentially a great kid, but at this point he became unusually quiet and withdrawn and spent a lot of time in his room or driving aimlessly around our new neighborhood. He was just trudging through the days, resigned to his new circumstances, but not finding anything to like about our new home. He had been putting up with this crap for four long years by now. As a twelve-year-old boy, when it's all over the papers that your father had sex with a sixteen-year-old girl—how mortifying! At that age, you don't even want to think about your parents having sex, much less with someone very near your age. Then this was followed by his father being arrested for soliciting a hooker. He wanted to escape all this, and soon found some friends at school to help him. His choice was to ignore schoolwork, hang out with his new buddies, and smoke weed or drink his concerns away.

I met some other parents at school events and games, but I remained distant. I was grieving the loss of my best friends and social network back home. Nobody could ever replace them; I wasn't even going to let anybody try. I shunned people. I'd left behind such a wonderful community in Massapequa. I knew I could never find better friends. I didn't want to get close to anybody ever again—it would just get taken away. I was cordial, but that was as far as it went. I preferred to stay to myself. Or with Joe—he was the only person I had.

I was utterly bereft. Our first few weeks in L.A., I would drop the kids at their schools, and then drive all the way out to the ocean. I'd sit there in my car and cry until it was time to pull myself together and pick the kids up. I knew I had to get it together for them, given that they'd been forced to give up everything they'd ever known. Joe could see I was not doing well. I found no joy in anything; I just did what I had to do to get through each day while constantly mourning the loss of my old life. Of course, in the hero role he was good at, he found a stable and encouraged me to go horseback riding. It perked me up briefly. Riding lessons at least gave me something to look forward to every week.

By Thanksgiving, I was getting urgent phone calls from Paul's new high school, reporting that he hadn't shown up for classes. Minor punishments like grounding didn't have any effect on his behavior. My sweet, funny, sensitive boy who had never caused me a moment's worry was now coming home obviously stoned or drunk, not even trying to hide it. I could easily see that he was spinning out of control. This new lifestyle wasn't working. As parents in a whole new state three thousand miles from home, Joe and I were just floundering. I knew my son was anesthetizing his grief because I was too. The only difference between us was that I was forty years old, and he was sixteen.

I could hardly blame him for wanting to escape however he could, but I was the mother, and I couldn't allow him to give up his life, despite my desire to do so. I had to make him care about his own life, even though I didn't care much about mine at the time. It was clear that he was headed down the path to failing or dropping out of high school and becoming a full-time drug addict. I couldn't even blame him. I understood what he was doing much better than he ever knew because all I wanted to do was withdraw and take my pills in peace. Paul was just a kid, though. For him and his fledgling life, I was going to put up a fight.

"Joe, we are going to lose him if we don't do something," I said. I wasn't exaggerating. I was frantic with worry. Joe agreed that whatever we needed to do, he would back me up.

I reached out to the mother of one of Paul's new friends and really poured out my worries to her. "He's not going to class, he's failing, and I know he's drinking and smoking pot all day, at the very least." She told me about a private school in Malibu with only eight or nine kids in each class. Lots of individualized instruction and plenty of attention were paid to each student. They offered structure and guidance, which, sadly, were both lacking in Paul's life. Joe simply wasn't capable of offering either—he was a loving father but more of a pal, the one the kids turned to for a good time and money. I probably didn't do enough given my own struggles with the move, but I did mobilize enough to find what I thought would be a good solution for our son.

This private school cost a fortune, but I didn't care. Paul started over in the middle of the school year, and I didn't care about that either. I didn't want him in his current school for another second. The new administration did what it promised, and Paul slowly but surely turned around. Oh, he still wasn't happy about the move, but he started making decent grades and going to class every day. He made a couple of close friends that he still has to this day—nice boys, who have grown into great young men. The Malibu school had a number of famous sons and daughters in attendance, so having the last name Buttafuoco wasn't nearly the big deal it had been in the Valley. *That* crisis, at least, seemed averted.

A year into our new life, money was getting tight. Joe had become very close to the owner of the Rainbow Room—he and his wife were wonderful to us—but it wasn't a career. Paul drove himself to his private school every day, and I wasn't sure I wanted Jessica in that same high school system that Paul had been so briefly and disastrously enrolled in.

We found a cute little house in the San Fernando Valley in a good neighborhood where Jessica could enter the local high school. The summer after eighth grade, I signed her up for a local acting workshop, and she made a couple of fast friends there. On the first day of high school, she knew only two people who would also be attending her new school that fall. Once again, she rose to the occasion, making a whole new group of friends and getting involved in all kinds of school activities with barely a pause.

Joe wanted to return to what he knew and was best at—auto body work—but he ran into a brick wall every time. No one wanted to hire him because of his notoriety, especially as an auto body guy. But eventually he met a man who took a liking to him, and they began working together. Joe excelled at bringing in customers and handing out cards all over town, as well as doing the actual body work and handling claims. Paul joined him at the business as soon as he was out of high school. His father brought him in, just as Cass had done with Joey twenty years before.

And Joe became very successful. He had the personality, the drive, and the work ethic to make that business profitable. He was doing quite well. I, meanwhile, was wallowing in self-pity, flying home every chance I got. I was still lost, but I didn't even want to be found. I didn't want to become involved with any of the other mothers or pursue horseback riding. The only time I was ever happy was on a plane ride to New York, where I stayed with my sister and saw my family. The first time I flew home for a visit, several months after our move, I absolutely couldn't wait to see all my friends in person again.

We met for a celebratory reunion lunch, and it was wonderful to see their faces, but hearing about their lives only made me feel left out and cheated. They were driving carpools, going to the beach club, getting involved with the high school PTA—in short, living the life I was supposed to be living! It hurt me so much to see what I had been forced to leave behind that I could no longer bear to stay in contact with them. I continued to return "home" frequently, but only visited with family from that point forward. I clung to them; they were all I had.

Sociopaths generally adjust quite easily to new environments. Whether it was jail on Long Island or the Rainbow Room in

Hollywood, Joe was perfectly at ease. To sociopaths, moving means nothing more than a fresh pool of people to size up and a brand-new set of circumstances to manipulate to their advantage. While I bitterly mourned my losses and struggled to find meaning in this strange new place—and help my equally lost son—I had to marvel at my husband's lack of feelings or concern for the loss of our entire lives. He wasn't looking back, and he certainly wasn't crying over spilled milk. I didn't know that there is no such thing as regret to a sociopath.

CHAPTER 8

REHABILITATION

Two full years into our "new life" in California, I was still very far from adjusting. I felt I had no purpose other than helping my two teenagers however I could. Jessica was very involved in high school activities, and it was probably all for the best that she needed me to drive her around all the time. At the very least, it gave me a reason to get up and have something to do. She was on the swim team, and we used to leave the house at five in the morning, when it was still pitch-black outside in the dead of winter, to get over to the college pool where her team practiced and held meets.

I would glance over at my full-of-life daughter, raring to go even at that ungodly hour, and think, *She's trying so hard, doing so well, how can I not?* I managed to get her everywhere she needed to be, but in the downtime I was a whole other story. As soon as I dropped her off, I'd return to a rented house that I had no desire to try to fix up. We had owned our own home since I was twenty-two years old, and I had always taken great pride in fixing up our houses: decorating, stenciling the walls, landscaping—you name it, I was a regular Martha Stewart. But who cared? This wasn't our house, so why bother? This would never be home to me.

Now that Paul and Jessie were teenagers with their own groups of friends and complicated social lives, I had plenty of free time when I wasn't chauffeuring. In the mornings, after I dropped Jessie off, I fell into the habit of coming home and crawling right back into bed, popping some pills, and zoning out in a pleasant haze. Half-awake, half-asleep, I'd watch TV all day until I knew everybody would be coming home for dinner. At that point, I managed to pull myself out of bed, make myself presentable, and appear reasonably together and alert for a game, event, or just making dinner and checking homework that night. It was a sad, lonely, but most of all boring time. I was forty-three years old, and it felt like my life was over. Depression and inertia hung over me like a fog. I functioned when necessary and did what I had to do, but that was all. I was anesthetized 24-7.

On one of my periodic trips home to New York—still the only activity in my life that excited me in any way—I was in the city and stopped by to say hello to Dominic Barbara, the man who'd long ago replaced Marvyn Kornberg and was still our attorney. We had become good friends. Dominic had seen me at my absolute lowest point—when Joe was arrested in Hollywood—and he'd cleaned up that mess the best he could. He was a very perceptive man, and he studied me carefully.

"You still taking all those pain pills, Mary Jo?" he asked.

"Yes, I am. I want to get off them, but I can't. A few hours without my medicine, and I'm sweating and shaking and falling apart. I don't want the kids to see me writhing around in pain in bed, going through withdrawal. I need to be around for them." I was long past getting high. I was taking thirty pills a day to stay "normal."

"I think you should go to a rehab center," he said matter-of-factly.

"No, no, I don't want to do that! A few days in a hospital, maybe, so they can wean me off these pills is what I need. I don't need rehab!"

"There's something else going on here besides your injury and the pain . . . you have some issues you need to deal with."

"Dominic, we don't even have health insurance. We live in a rented house, and we have to think about Jessica and college. I can't afford rehab, even if I needed it, which I don't." That was the end of that discussion as far as I was concerned.

"I will pay, Mary Jo, if you are willing to go into treatment. You're out in California now, near the Betty Ford Center, and they're really the best. It will be my gift to you."

This was an incredibly generous and kind offer, but I was balking big-time. Just the word "rehab" brought up terrible memories of the years of Joe's cocaine abuse. I was responsible, I took care of my children, and I didn't sell a house to a cocaine dealer! I got my pills from the doctor because I had a bullet in my skull and unrelenting pain! Sure, I needed to stop taking quite so many pills, but basically I was fine. Joe was the addict, not me! I didn't need to do anything as drastic as Betty

Ford! Jessica was in school and still needed me, and I didn't want any more press scrutiny . . . I had lots of reasons why I couldn't go. Dominic wouldn't let the matter drop, so I called the Betty Ford Center and they mailed me some information. I examined it. Joe and I talked it over; he was very supportive. He didn't like seeing me so depressed, not wanting to go anywhere or do anything, spending half my days curled up under the covers. Betty Ford was booked solid with a long waiting list, but Dominic pulled some strings and got me a place with very little notice. He called me one night.

"You're in. You can check in this Monday, but you have to go now. It's a thirty-day program, and I will take care of the bills. You really do need to do this, Mary Jo." The ball was suddenly in motion. I was going into treatment. My main concern was that this would become another tabloid news story. I could just see the headlines. Just imagining it sent waves of shame and embarrassment over me. I didn't want anyone to know my life had sunk to this new low. I agreed to go, but only if I could register under a different last name.

On a blazingly hot day in August of 1998, Joey drove me through the desert to the world-renowned treatment facility in Rancho Mirage. I sat next to him, absolutely petrified of what was to come. I couldn't even speak. I was so sad and bewildered. How had my life come to this? I was in California, where I never wanted to live, and Joey was driving me to rehab? I popped one last big handful of pills as we parked the car, then followed my husband reluctantly as he walked into the main building.

Right from the start, it was one of the most humbling experiences of my life. I didn't want to be there in the first place, so I certainly wasn't feeling or acting grateful for this opportunity or hopeful about my recovery. They didn't care what my attitude was. I was now part of a very well-oiled machine, and there was nothing—especially an attitude problem—that they hadn't seen or dealt with before. Joe left, and I was left to the assembly-line admissions process. They were quite efficient. Every person who arrived each day was just one of a new batch, and I went through the whole admissions day with a random group of strangers. After some paperwork in the main office, the five of us who were checking in that day were shuttled onto a golf cart for a short ride to the hospital on the grounds. A man who couldn't have weighed more than eighty pounds, so out of it he was transferred to the cart in a wheelchair, was propped up next to me. His arms were covered with fresh needle marks and bruises. I edged away and thought to myself, *I am in the wrong place. I don't belong here with these people.*

The hospital workup was very thorough. I, of course, had a more complicated medical history than most. Every conceivable test was run on me, which took quite a few hours. Every single item I had brought was examined. Nail polish, perfume, hair spray, mouthwash—they were all confiscated. As the day wore on, I became increasingly antsy. The effects of the pills wore off and the dreaded anxious, sweaty feeling of panic came over me. I needed another dose. I certainly wasn't going to get one there. I grew weaker and more nauseous as the day wore on, and my blood pressure eventually dropped to a dangerously low level. The doctors gave me some sort of medicine—not nearly enough for my tolerance level—but the immediate physiological problem was addressed.

The five or six days that followed were sheer hell. All I wanted to do was roll into a ball in bed. I had uncontrollable shakes and vomited constantly. When I wasn't throwing up, my mouth was so dry I could barely swallow, let alone eat. I woke up each morning drenched in sweat, the sheets soaking wet, which the staff had anticipated. I'd been given extra sheets on my first day, and the first order of business each morning at 6:00 AM was for me to remake my bed. I was barely able to stand up, but rules were rules. The program was the same for everybody, though I did not want to follow it. "I just need to get this stuff out of my body. I don't need to do all this other crap. I want to get out of here and go home. I don't belong here!" I kept telling anyone who'd listen.

"Oh, no, you definitely need this program. Stick it out," the counselors told me. I dragged myself to the main office and literally begged the head counselors to excuse me from group meetings. "Please, I can't do these meetings. I don't want to get into why I'm here and have everybody staring at me because of who I am. I'm here because Amy Fisher shot me in the head and I take too many pills!"

They had heard it all many times before and didn't care. "You're going to go to every meeting along with everybody else." Every day we followed a strict schedule, with several group meetings that, sick as a dog, I was compelled to attend. "Come on, come on, you're not dying here," the counselor would say. No, it only felt like I was. I hated every minute. They might force me to sit there, but I wasn't about to say anything. The first week I was so miserable that I couldn't have spoken if I'd wanted to. I sat, and sweat, and listened, and mainly thought about how much I hated being there. I didn't know if anyone recognized me, and if they did I was too out of it to care. Many of the other group members were equally shaky. My identity was the last thing anyone cared about as they detoxed. The staff knew who I was, of course, but they were accustomed to public figures as patients.

Somewhere around a week or ten days into the program, I simply gave up the fight and surrendered to the process. It was relentless. The program took up every waking minute, and I couldn't escape. Accepting the reality that I needed to be there came easier once I could actually eat, keep food down, and the cold sweats stopped as the last of the drugs drained from my system. After six or seven days, I was clean for the first time since I'd been shot. Tired, shaky, and weak, but completely drug-free. I stopped begrudging the early wake-up, the endless chores, and the round of meetings, where I listened to some truly horrifying stories of loss from other women. The ones who had lost their children due to drug and alcohol abuse particularly moved me. The fact that every life had problems, many much worse than mine, was made very clear to me several times a day. After a completely silent couple of weeks, where I simply shook my head when it was my turn to speak, all my resistance vanished one afternoon when I felt compelled to finally talk.

We were in another endless meeting about getting to the roots of addiction—why we drank or abused drugs—when all my years of pent-up anger exploded. I had been living with it for so long that it was simply a part of me. Even I was amazed at the depths of my rage as it spilled out. "I hate that bitch Amy Fisher . . . it's all her fault!" I screamed. "I was minding my own business, and she destroyed my entire life. She ruined my health, she ruined my husband's life—he had to go to jail because of her lies!—and she ruined my children's lives, too!"

This gave us all something to talk about for quite a while. After letting me rant until I was exhausted—me, me, me and all that had been done so unfairly to *me*—the counselor spoke up. "Well, what do you want to do about this? You have every right to be angry, but do you want to spend the rest of your life feeling like this, living like this, not wanting to get out of bed every day and blunting your anger with pills instead of dealing with those feelings?"

Well, this was something to consider. Over the next two weeks, I worked through many complicated layers of rage that I'd held so closely for so long. Everything I was so angry about—the loss of my whole life—I relived, sober. It was very painful. At one point, I was assigned an exercise to write a letter to Amy—one that would never be mailed—telling her exactly how I felt. For hours, I sat, stone-cold sober, and reconsidered the chaos of the past six years. As I wrote down how I felt, everything poured out of me in a letter filled with vitriol.

My counselor read the letter. At the end, she said, "All right. Do you want to continue to carry this anger, or are you willing to learn some tools to help you manage this anger and live with what's happened, and get on with the rest of your life? You're only in your forties, with a lot of years to live ahead of you. How are you going to live them?" I really *didn't* want to live this way anymore. I was miserable and had been for years. At an outdoor group ceremony that evening, all the patients took turns dropping their letters into a campfire. As each turned to ash, we all cheered for its writer. The literal burning away of years of resentment, regrets, and pain symbolized the idea that this was to be our new beginning.

Through the many workshops and programs that followed, I learned—slowly and painfully—to let certain feelings go. I had to learn acceptance of things I could not change, a very hard lesson for me. In addition to my rage at Amy, I had plenty of leftover anger about the fact that I had never been given my due as the victim of a violent crime. The media had turned it into The Joey and Amy Show, the police and prosecutors hadn't helped, and the whole experience had left me deeply scarred and resentful. I had to come to terms with the fact that I couldn't change or fix any of it. It was scary. If I let go of my anger, what was I going to do with myself? The wheels started to turn. A tremendous shift began. I was letting go.

I had to mourn for everything that I had lost without the buffering of any pills. For days, I was grief-stricken as I relived all my losses and faced all these feelings raw. There was nowhere to go and no pill to pop to make it all blurry. It was as big an awakening for me as the day I opened my eyes to see the lights and the nurse hovering over me in the hospital.

I walked out of the Betty Ford Center with a gold "one day at a time" medallion in my hand, a clear head, and a better attitude than I'd had in years. I was detoxed but knew I had plenty of work still to do. It wasn't easy to let go of the anger that had been barely contained for so many years, but I was calm and determined. "What happened, happened; this is your life now. What are you going to do with it now that you're free?" The counselors' words rang in my ears.

I returned home to my little rented house in Los Angeles and faced life sober. It was a tremendous relief to be free of the pill habit. I never even considered abusing them again. The pain in my head, particularly problems with my right ear, was always present, but manageable. I looked better, felt better, and had a new attitude.

I continued to work on my anger issues by reciting mantras to myself and practicing calming breathing exercises when I felt the old anger start to flare up. I lived the 12-step philosophy the best I could. I continued to read all kinds of books on forgiveness and became very clear on what I was doing here:

forgiving, not condoning. Amy's act was never going to be comprehensible or excusable in any way, but for my own peace of mind I had to free myself of the hatred I felt for her. From now on, I had to concentrate on looking ahead and dealing with the life I had—not the one I missed. I was working my program, as they say in recovery circles.

Joe and Paul were busy with work at the new auto body shop. Jessica was in school, with friends, or playing sports, and everything seemed to be working itself out. I was working through my grief and feeling lighter every day, as if a huge burden was slowly lifting—one I hadn't consciously realized I was carrying. I started to really consider *me* again, not what had been done to me, but the active, social person I'd been before the shooting. I knew I'd never be the same woman again, but I was certainly capable of making some kind of contribution or difference to someone beyond my immediate family. I believed again that I was worth something.

My first step was to get busy; I needed to find something to do to fill my time. No more lying around a darkened bedroom all day. I saw a notice seeking volunteers to record books on tape for the blind, so I signed up for the program. It was a baby step, something to get me out of the house each day, but I was surprised at how much I enjoyed the work. Each day when I showed up, I was given whatever needed to be recorded that day, ranging from college textbooks on astronomy, to Harlequin romances, to serious biographies. I learned how to master the huge reel-to-reel machines and conduct a recording session on my own. Sitting in the booth with the headphones on, I'd get lost in another world. And I certainly learned about some things I'd never have known otherwise. When I left each session, I took some satisfaction from the realization that I had done something good and productive, no matter how small, that might brighten someone's day a bit, or even help educate them.

Less than four months after my return home, I got a phone call one afternoon out of the blue from Dominic Barbara informing me that Roseanne Fisher, Amy Fisher's mother, had hired a new attorney named Bruce Barket. My stomach clenched. I wasn't sure what was coming next.

"Roseanne Fisher would like to meet with you personally. Would you be willing to come out here and do that?"

I would never pass up a trip home. "Sure," I said. I didn't even think about it, especially when I learned it wouldn't be on my dime. I had no particular desire or curiosity to meet Amy's mother, but I jumped at any chance to go home. Joe couldn't have been more supportive. "I think you should go. It's a great idea. It will be good for you. Go ahead."

"Are you sure, Joe?"

"Absolutely. It's closure, and you need it. Go!" he said. He could not have been more encouraging.

I felt perfectly confident going into that meeting with Roseanne at Dominic's office on Long Island. In fact, I felt a bit self-righteous. *Hey, my kids don't run around shooting people in the head* was my mean-spirited thought. I recollected the one time I'd seen Roseanne face-to-face, during Amy's original sentencing, and I had given her and Mr. Fisher the most evil glare I could manage. I hated them. They had clearly fallen down on the job. Seven years later, with my own teenagers, I felt more forgiving, but still a bit smug.

I arrived first, and when Roseanne came into the room, she walked over to me and held out her hand. I extended myself and gave her a hug. Seeing her really jolted me. We were the exact same age, only a few months apart, but she looked like an old, worn-out woman. She was painfully thin. I could feel all the bones in her shoulder and back when I hugged her. For the first time, I thought about how devastating this had been for her. She was a mother, after all, and now I had an eighteen-year-old with his own problems. They were nothing like Amy's, of course, but I definitely had a new perspective.

I suddenly remembered going to visit Joe in jail, the long, humiliating wait in line, the dehumanizing search, the horrible institutional setting. I pictured this small, defeated woman going to visit her only child for seven years, week after week, hours away in upstate New York. I was flooded with pity. For the first time I looked at her with empathy. We sat down, and I soon found myself trying to put Roseanne at ease because she was so nervous and so sorry. She apologized over and over. "What made Amy like this?" I asked, honestly trying to understand what had gone so wrong.

She didn't know, but the stories she told me that day went a long way toward explaining at least some of Amy's behavior.

Roseanne had been a shy eighteen-year-old girl with strict Italian parents fresh off the boat. When she started dating Mr. Fisher—a divorced Jewish man almost twenty years her senior—they told her in the strongest possible terms to find someone else because they did not approve. She defied her parents' wishes and married him anyway. Amy was born a year later.

In a trembling voice, Roseanne described how Mr. Fisher had been verbally and physically abusive toward both of them. At some point I had to interrupt and say, "Why didn't you leave?"

"I tried," she said almost inaudibly. "When Amy was two, I went back home, and my parents said to me, 'You made your bed, you lie in it. You did this; you're not coming back here. This is not our problem.'" With nowhere to go, she went back to her house and abusive husband. Her stories were heartrending. Most of me felt nothing but pity. Still, the angry, judgmental part of my mind asked, *How could you let your kid grow up in that environment?* The Fishers had divorced shortly after Amy went to prison, but it was too late for their daughter. Still, who was I to say or judge her behavior?

The visit went well, I thought. We hugged again when we parted. I had no desire to see Roseanne again or to be her friend, but I felt good about the whole situation. It was refreshing to be healed enough to open my mind and think more about other people, how badly they'd been affected, and what they were going through. In my hurt and anger, I hadn't spared a thought for Amy or her mother. Now I had to face how badly other families were hurting as well, how many people's lives were forever changed.

Several days after I returned home, a letter from Roseanne arrived in the mail. She thanked me for seeing her and told me I was a wonderful person, a saint, how great I was, and so on. It was very sweet. A week passed, and a call came in from Bruce Barket. "I have a letter for you," he said. "It's a letter from Amy. She's very sorry about what happened, and she has written you to apologize. May I send it to you?"

"I've been waiting seven years for this," I said in surprise. "I've been waiting seven years for that girl to say she's sorry."

"Well, she has written you this letter, and I hope you'll read it . . . so can I send it?"

"Of course, of course," I said. "I'm interested to hear what she has to say." I was stunned and curious. I had never imagined this day would come. A few days later, a long handwritten letter arrived in the mail. Amy's letter was quite vague, as she was in prison and not allowed to refer to many things or use certain words. But the language was heartfelt, and she clearly apologized. The whole incident was her fault. Joe had had nothing to do with it. She had many issues she was working on that she'd tell me about someday, and she was very, very sorry. She had always wanted to say she was sorry, she wrote, but had been advised by former counsel not to reach out to me.

It has taken a long time to realize exactly how serious what I did was and what factors in my life led me to it. I don't have the benefit of professional help in prison for a va-

riety of reasons, but my mom helps me a lot. She said she met you and you weren't what she expected. Mom told me you were a nice, kind person. I've always tried to think you were mean and horrible because it was easier for me to deal with what I did to you. When my mom was talking about you I became filled with emotions that I had never felt before. I wanted to meet you and tell you in person how bad I feel for everything that has happened. I'm not sure if you'll ever believe that I'm sorry for what I did to you, but I am. I had a lot of anger inside of me and I directed it at you. That anger wasn't for you and I know now that what I did to you is the worst thing one human being can do to another.

Tears ran down my face. *At last—a seemingly sincere apology from the person who had harmed me.* She was finally taking responsibility for the devastation she had wrought on so many lives. *Thank you. Thank you for owning up to this and apologizing at last.*

Shortly after receiving the letter, Bruce Barket filed a brief seeking a new trial for Amy on the grounds that her personal relationship with her counsel Eric Naiburg constituted a conflict of interest, which had interfered with his ability to properly represent her. Amy claimed in her brief that while she was out on bail, they had kissed, touched, and acted out his sexual fantasies. Dozens of poems, notes, and letters Eric had written to Amy over the years were attached as proof. They were certainly damning.

My old nemesis, Assistant District Attorney Fred Klein, officially notified me that based on overwhelming evidence of Eric Naiburg's misconduct, they were granting Amy Fisher a new trial. The DA's office planned to negotiate some sort of settlement rather than go through the time and expense of an entire trial. I had been forced to let go of my desire to have my day in court years before. Once again, all kinds of deals were being made behind the scenes. However, I was consulted, and this time I was able to participate in the process without rage or painkillers clouding my judgment.

Their new proposal was this: to reduce the original sentence of five to fifteen years to three to twelve years. With seven years' time already served, there was an excellent chance she would get out on parole.

I reacted to this news with very mixed feelings. "What do you think, Joey?" I asked.

"Whatever you decide," Joey answered. "Whatever you think best, I'm behind you. If you want to accept this sentence reduction, good for you. Whatever it takes for closure."

I flew back to New York for a behind-closed-doors meeting with the district attorney's office. I reconciled myself to the idea of Amy being let out of prison, but I wanted certain stipulations to go along with her probation. If she was going to be let out, her four-year probation wasn't going to be a picnic. She would have a curfew of 8:00 PM, drug testing, and be prohibited from going to bars and nightclubs. She would have to get a job and live with her mother. I really thought that she would be unable to live with these terms. She would mess up fast once she was let out. How do you tell a twenty-five-year-old who's been locked up for seven years—or any person at any age who's been locked up for years, for that matter—not to go out at night?

As I wrangled through all these arrangements with the attorneys, my attitude was resignation. She's going to get out, but at least let her get out with conditions attached. Eventually, all the terms were agreed upon, a court date was set for April 21, 1999, and I returned home to California. The rumblings in the press began. Mary Jo was forgiving Amy Fisher, and she was going to be let out! Amy would be free! Mary Jo was returning to the scene where it all began to face Amy in court again! All the TV shows were calling, *People* magazine wanted to do a story with me, and the Long Island press was salivating over the story.

Joe didn't want to attend—he would stay home with the kids, and my parents would attend the hearing for moral support—but he offered unqualified support. I had one last talk with my husband and kids before I left for the court hearing. "Is everybody all right with this decision?" I asked.

"Whatever you want, we're behind you," they assured me. I got on the plane and braced myself for the media onslaught on the other end. As the limo drove me through the city to my hotel, I asked the driver to turn on the local news. The horrifying slaughter at Columbine High School in Colorado was on every station. Nothing of this magnitude had ever happened in an American school before. I was no longer a big deal. Suddenly, Amy's court hearing was relegated to page five. I was left in relative peace for my entire stay. The news media had a much more important story to report.

Matters proceeded smoothly and as planned at Amy's hearing. Amy cried as she spoke. She reiterated that the shooting had been all her idea, that nobody else, particularly Joe, was involved, and that she was very sorry. In turn, I made a beautiful speech saying that I knew she hadn't realized that I was somebody's mother, somebody's child, and somebody's sister at the time of the shooting. I was alive. I had been given a second chance, and I was giving Amy that same opportunity. Seven years after the fact, I was finally getting what I had wanted all along: the victim and the perpetrator facing each other in a courtroom and each getting their say. It was time for Fred Klein to speak. "Your honor," he began, "I just want it to be known that the prosecution of Joseph Buttafuoco for the rape of Amy Fisher . . ."

I was instantly flooded with shock and outrage—first to hear Joe's name at all, then to hear it in the context of rape. Once again, this was my day, and it was all about the same old circus sideshow.

～

I arrived back in California and was surprised to hear from the kids that Joey had gone to Las Vegas for a quick trip while I was back East. Yes, they were nineteen and sixteen years old, perfectly capable of looking out for themselves, but I was a worrier.

"Vegas—what were you doing there? Didn't you watch the case on television?" I asked.

"Oh, I just decided to go with a few of the guys, last-minute, a quick break. Why would I watch *that* on television?" he wanted to know.

Just that fast, there was a subtle but noticeable change in his attitude. This comment wasn't like him. It certainly wasn't particularly supportive not to even watch the highlights on CNN. I was hurt, but brushed it off. My main concern was the kids.

"Joey, how could you leave them? What if one of the kids had been in an accident?"

"Come on, they were fine. We're all fine! Quit worrying so much!"

In making it through rehab, meeting with Roseanne, and very publicly forgiving Amy Fisher, I had directed more of my attention and energy to my personal needs and well-being than I had in decades—since I got married, in fact. Joe and I had been a perfect match. For years, I had been an ideal, willing victim. Unconsciously or not, Joe sensed my new strength, and when a sociopath has completely worn out one willing victim, he will look for a fresh victim to meet and charm.

The next afternoon, there was a knock on the front door. Ever since I'd been shot, I hated unannounced knocks on the door. In fact, I refused to answer them. If I didn't know someone was coming over at a certain time, forget it—I wasn't going

to let them in. Paul, however, opened the door. A tabloid reporter from the *Globe* identified herself and asked to speak to
me. I figured she was looking for a quote about Amy's imminent release. "Would you care to comment about Joey and his
new girlfriend who accompanied him on a recent trip to Las
Vegas?" she asked.

This was how I learned about Evanka.

CHAPTER 9

GUMPTION JUNCTION

I was used to this kind of crap from the media. I shut the door in the reporter's face and turned to snap at Paul. "What have I told you about opening the door?" The fact that he answered an unexpected knock at the door was much more my concern at the time than any provocative remark a reporter might make to catch me off guard to try to get a quote. I'd been playing that game for years by this time. I wasn't going to fall for their tricks so easily.

When Joe came home from work that night, I asked him about it. "Oh, Evanka? She's just a friend. A customer. Paulie knows her. I was with the guys . . . we ran into her in Vegas . . . turned out we were staying at the same hotel. Someone snapped a picture, you know how people do. I guess someone sold it to the tabloids to get some cash." He wasn't the slightest bit rattled. The sociopath always has a story.

Several days later, Amy was released from prison on probation and returned to her mother's home. There was a brief media flurry as the press followed her around for a few days, but she was keeping a surprisingly low profile. I didn't much care. Amy Fisher free on Long Island? Good luck to her—*I* couldn't stay there, and I hadn't even done anything wrong!

Several weeks later, I was back in New York finalizing some legal matters at Bruce Barket's office. He pulled out a copy of the *Globe* and said jokingly, "So, what's this about Joey and a girlfriend?" He handed me the paper, and we both studied the picture of Joey next to a voluptuous woman. It was hardly incriminating. They were just standing there side by side with other people surrounding them, though the article did in fact detail that Joey had checked into the Rio Hotel on Friday night—a hotel Joey and I had stayed in together on numerous occasions.

"I don't know," Bruce said. "It's probably nothing . . . you know this is what the tabloids do . . . they could snap a picture like this of me and you!" It wasn't pleasant to read this story, but after all we'd been through with the media, I couldn't take it too seriously.

Still, the incident was out there, a lingering shadow in the back of my mind. Meanwhile, the lease on our little rented house was ending, and we had enough money put aside to buy a home. Joey was doing very well at work—well enough to buy a house in Los Angeles. When the house-hunting process started, Joey acquired a new and very unwelcome attitude, one I'd never been exposed to before. "You did what you wanted to; now I'm going to do what I want to."

I went to check out lots of houses and found several I

thought were viable. All we needed was a three-bedroom house in decent shape—no more fixer-uppers for me—in a decent neighborhood, maybe with a nice little yard. I called him a few times to ask him to come take a look, but he didn't like anything I found. Somewhere in his travels he had stumbled across an absolute monstrosity of a property way out in Chatsworth, a remote Valley suburb. Possibly it had once been a beautiful, elegant home, but that had been in the distant past. The place was an abandoned wreck surrounded by overgrown plantings and crumbling outbuildings. It had been foreclosed by the bank and sat empty for years, maybe decades, growing more uninhabitable and neglected as the years passed. Joey became obsessed with it.

He took me to tour the property. The main house was probably six thousand square feet—absolutely ridiculous for a family of four. It was a huge pile of stone with ornate iron shutters rusting all over the windows and balconies. I hated it on sight. "We do not need this," I said. "Forget what it costs. Imagine what it takes just to heat this place. And keeping up the grounds! Not to mention it needs new everything!"

"I've talked to the bank. I can get it for a song. It's going to be great!" Joey was bubbling over with his usual enthusiasm. But I was much older, wiser, and, quite frankly, a lot more tired than I used to be. We didn't need it, I didn't want it, and this time I wasn't going to go along with the latest over-the-top purchase and spend my life in some horrible fixer-upper—just as the kids were growing up and leaving us, too. It was perfectly obvious this property was nothing but a money pit.

For twenty-some-odd years, all I'd ever heard from Joey were variations on one theme. "I'm sorry. I love you. I need you. Whatever you want. You're right." It was a well-worn pattern. We both had our roles to play, and mine was the voice of reason. His was to agree with me and promise whatever I wanted to hear. All of a sudden, Joe dug in his heels. "You did what you wanted about Amy. I want this house, and I can afford it. I'm getting it." There was quite a lot of "I" going on all of a sudden, when I was accustomed to "we." This entitlement game he was suddenly playing had come out of left field. We were talking about a house, not forgiving Amy Fisher—a decision he had fully backed. "Joe, I asked you twenty times. We discussed it on numerous occasions. I wanted your opinion. I asked you over and over what you thought I should do and how you felt about the whole situation. All you said was 'Whatever you want.' You absolutely encouraged me to get closure. Now that the whole matter is behind us, and I actually did something for me that needed to be done and I feel good about it, you're going to throw it in my face?"

"You should never have forgiven her . . . I never will!" This was news to me. The minute I'd publicly forgiven her, he was suddenly furious—at Amy and at me. I hadn't heard anything like this before. All I knew was that he was displeased, it was my fault, and my forgiving Amy Fisher had somehow become his excuse to move ahead on a house purchase without my agreement. It was now time for Joe to do what he wanted (as if he hadn't been all along!). He could attempt to justify this insane purchase by claiming it was "his turn," but I wasn't buying it. I felt stronger and freer and not chained to anger and the past since I'd forgiven Amy Fisher. I didn't want this house, and I wasn't going along with it.

When it became clear that he was going to buy this house no matter what I said, Joe accompanied me to the bank where he had finagled some deal to buy the property. I flat-out refused to cosign the mortgage, so the bank had me sign a quit-claim agreement stating that the property was his alone and I had no financial responsibility for it—a rather unusual situation for a couple who'd been married for twenty-two years. "I don't want to be responsible for this, Joe. I don't want my name anywhere near it. It's a bad idea." But Joey didn't care what I thought. I couldn't imagine where the large down payment he produced had even come from, no matter how well the shop was doing, but it wasn't my problem. I refused to allow any of this to become my problem.

Jessica was entering the eleventh grade in the fall, and Paul was working at the shop every day with his father. Our family moved into the new house in July 1999. I lived there for less than six months.

My wonderfully loving and supportive husband turned on a dime with the new house purchase. Looking back, it's clear to me that his relationship with Evanka had already started. We'd had nothing but strain in our lives since the shooting.

Quite frankly, both of us were worn-out. I could even under-stand the allure of a fresh relationship in which you weren't constantly rehashing the last twenty-five years. But instead of saying to me that he was feeling a little bit different, or that he needed something more or new from our marriage, he acted on his whims. He wandered off and did exactly as he pleased.

By this point in my marriage and my life, I didn't much care what he did. I had resigned myself to this marriage for several years now. Every time I had tried to leave in the past, Joe had pulled out all the stops to get me to stay. Always, the scene in the restaurant with Jessica four years earlier on Long Island was never far from my mind. I had given up the idea of ever going—resigned to my fate is the only way to put it. Instead of leaving, I had chosen to try to work on myself—by getting off the pills and getting in the right frame of mind to even be willing and able to meet Roseanne and eventually forgive Amy.

Joey was energized by the new property and spent a lot of time working on it. He threw tons of money into remodeling and fixing it up. He was constantly renovating something, in-cluding a private apartment with its own entrance for Paul. I refused to do a thing. I did not give a damn about this black hole of a huge drafty house. All my modern furniture looked ridiculous in this old Spanish hacienda-style place. I privately thought it resembled nothing more than a Mexican brothel, but hey, it wasn't mine. I didn't bother to give any input on decorating.

I was free of the fog of pills, and I was at peace with my

decision about Amy. Now, clearly, I had troubles in my marriage, but I couldn't seem to work up much interest in fixing them. We never fought, we rarely even raised our voices, but we also barely spoke. The two of us never went out together or spent time alone at home with each other anymore. We were two cordial strangers sharing a house. Paul was nineteen years old, and Jessica sixteen. What was I hanging on for? By Thanksgiving, I had had it. "Joe," I told him days before the long holiday weekend, "I think I'm going to leave. This just isn't working."

For the first time in nearly twenty-five years, Joe replied calmly, "I think you're right." His words were a tremendous shock. "Separation is a good idea." I was taken aback by this calm reaction, but we continued the discussion and resolved to get through the holidays together—until New Year's, to be precise—then I would make my announcement and find somewhere new to live. "Go look for your own place," Joe said at the end of our talk. "Whatever you want, go find it and get it. I will take care of you."

I started searching for my own place during the day, and I found a cute two-bedroom apartment in Woodland Hills. I was very concerned about minimizing the impact of our separation on Jessica. Paul was an adult now, working for a living and involved with his own girlfriend, so I wasn't too worried about him. But I still wanted to cushion and protect Jessica as much as possible.

Apartment-hunting and planning my exit over the next six weeks was a strange, sad time for me, knowing I was leaving, and knowing that Joey didn't care if I left. As always, I worried about the press. I didn't want it out there that we were officially separating—at last, many would say—because of Jessica, more than anything else. Our interactions at this time were very amicable; there was no fighting, just resignation on both our parts. It wasn't working for either of us. I had grown tired of the fights, the drama, and the overcontemplation of our situation. I had truly begun to not only grasp the concept of accepting the things I could not change, but was ready to practice it. I was ready to move on to the action phase of my personal change.

That New Year's Eve, I made a decision I regret very much to this day. "You tell Jessica about the separation," I told Joe. Of course, we should have broken the news to her together, but at the time I just couldn't stand the idea of hurting her or letting her down. He did tell her, on New Year's Day 2000. Joe took our daughter outside for a private talk, and when they came back into the house, shock and confusion were written all over her face. She looked like the wind had been completely knocked out of her—which, in a sense, it had been. After her outburst in the restaurant, I had purposely protected and insulated her from any feelings I had of personal unhappiness or dissatisfaction with her father from that point on; she had enough to deal with. This was literally a bolt from the blue to our daughter.

"This is going to be fun, Jessica! You'll have two places to stay, and there's a pool in my new place and racquetball, and you'll have your own room at my apartment." I was trying to make the best of the situation, chattering on nervously, when I should have just been quiet. Jessica couldn't say a word; she was too stunned to speak. Paul didn't have much to say about it at all, but as always, he was stoic and held his emotions. The news was broken—it was official. I was finally leaving.

I had never lived on my own—not once in my entire life. I went directly from my parents' house to the first house Joey and I saved for and bought together. For the first time in my life, I was *alone*. Apartment living was a big adjustment for me. All the things every college kid knows were a mystery to me. The first time I used the community laundry, I accidentally grabbed a neighbor's pile of clothes and took it up to my apartment, and they had to come looking for it. At forty-four, I was learning how to live by myself. Joe and I had cosigned the lease, and he was very agreeable to making the monthly rent payment. My new apartment was only six miles from Joe's house, and Jessica was welcome to stay at either place, whichever was easiest for her. Instead of being exhilarating, living on my own was anticlimactic. I was forced to acknowledge that the fight was over.

For years, I had been fighting tooth and nail to hold things together. All that energy and effort had come to nothing. Here I was three thousand miles from home, forty-four years old, alone, financially dependent on Joe, in an apartment in the

Valley, of all places. All the strength I'd gathered over the past couple of years by getting clean and off pills, settling the Amy Fisher matter, and so on seemed to evaporate in the anonymous apartment building. I sat alone and wondered, once again, how my life had come to this. Who was I . . . and where the hell was I headed?

The time had come to make the phone call I dreaded—to my parents. Since we'd moved to California, I'd never told my parents how bad things had gotten for me. We spoke on the phone frequently, but I always just said, "Oh, fine, fine, everything is fine here." Even when I lived two miles away from them, I had done my best to keep my problems just that—my own problems. I wasn't going to start unloading all my troubles at this point!

Now I had no choice because they would need my new phone number and address. My mother had mellowed considerably in recent years, but at that time I was still very fearful of her reaction. I gathered my courage, dialed her number, and finally told her, "Mom, I've left Joe. I had to. Our marriage wasn't working out. It hasn't been working for a long time." Her immediate reaction was anger and disapproval.

"This is what happens when you don't have God in your life!" she said. This was an old, old battle between us. She constantly reminded me that I was a living miracle and how hard so many people had prayed for me when I was shot. She believed I should be thanking God every day for sparing me, preferably at daily Mass. It drove her crazy that I didn't attend church regularly, to the point that I finally just asked her to stop talking about it. But it all came pouring out again with this news.

"A marriage involves three people . . . the husband, the wife, and God!" she said. On and on she went in this vein. It was a long lecture. I sat in my lonely apartment three thousand miles away and felt visibly smaller and more hurt as the minutes passed. I was so down already, so shaky about living alone . . . this was not what I needed. Not at all. Her disapproval was what I feared and dreaded and did my best to avoid for years, and it all came raining down just when I was at my lowest. As she continued to rant, I started to get angry and defensive.

"You're kidding me, right?" I finally said. "You're not here . . . you don't see what's going on! This situation has nothing to do with going to church!" It was fruitless. By the time we hung up, I was absolutely furious. I called my sister Jeanne, crying and angry at the same time. She sympathized, listened to me, and did her best to make me feel better. I hung up and immediately called my other sister Eileen, who was also wonderful. If nothing else, they both understood how my mother could be when she was upset and got on a roll. "I'm not calling her again," I told Eileen before we hung up. "She can call me!"

And damned if that phone ever rang again. She didn't call, and I absolutely refused to call her. As the days and weeks passed, it became a Mexican standoff. A deep melancholy overtook me. I had my own place, and I'd finally left Joe, but I couldn't seem to find the interest or energy to do something—

anything—else. I made a conscious decision to let all the friends we'd made in California—not that there were many, but I had a few—go with Joe. I gradually faded out of the picture and let everybody stay in touch with him—the fun half of the couple. Now that I was free to do what I pleased, I didn't want to do anything except sleep. I was very, very tired.

Jessica was so busy with her school events and sports teams that I didn't see much of her. She was old enough to drive herself where she needed to go. I made sure to pull myself together when she was around—usually at night. My apartment was close to her high school, so she generally spent weeknights with me. Usually I went to bed early with a bottle of wine, drank it until I fell asleep, and mourned the end of life as I knew it—again.

Every sad song on the radio reminded me of Joe and the many good times we'd shared going all the way back to high school. That had been the hardest part of getting away—the good times had been so great, and no matter what, he'd always professed undying love and adoration for me. I sat alone in my little apartment on beautiful sunny California days and cried for hours. I was absolutely grief-stricken. I had gotten away, but I was badly wounded. Not to put too fine a point on it, I wallowed in self-pity. One weekend I knew Jessica was spending the weekend with her father. My big plan for Friday night was to go to the local Albertson's grocery story, buy a bottle of wine, come home, and drink it. By myself.

I put on a baseball cap and chose my bottle at the store. It was all I bought—a pretty sad, lonely, single purchase. As I stood at the counter paying, the cashier said to me, "Are you Mary Jo Buttafuoco?"

"Yeah, guilty," I half joked.

"Oh. My. God! I admire you so much!" the woman said. She went on and on. "You have been through so much, and you've handled it so well! What a beautiful example of forgiveness you've set. You're such a kind human being." She could not have been nicer or sweeter. "You are such an inspiration!" she exclaimed.

Some inspiration. I stood there listening, almost squirming, thinking, *If she only knew.* I was a mess. I was heading home to drink an entire bottle of wine alone in bed, and she thought I was an inspiration. I thanked her and took that bottle of wine to the car, where I sat for a minute and reflected on how ironic that encounter had been. A total stranger thought I was great. I didn't feel great about me; I felt like a total failure. I was just getting through the days, drinking and crying myself to sleep at night. I had survived, but for what?

A good four months after I left Joe, my mother finally called, as if we had spoken the week before. "Hi, haven't talked to you for a while—what's going on?" she asked. I was shocked, but went along with the game. Neither of us mentioned our previous conversation. We pretended that nothing had happened and resumed our regular talks, but she had no idea how bad off I was. No one did.

Jessica, Paul, and even Joe had no idea that I was an absolute wreck, broken inside. Joe remained very cordial, paying the bills without a question, and became openly involved with his new girlfriend, Evanka. She was a thirty-something divorcée with a young son, and she demanded a great deal of Joe's time and attention. I never met her and didn't know anything about her personally except what I heard about her from the kids. It was clear that she was "high-maintenance." I didn't really care. She had had nothing to do with my leaving. Joey swore up and down until well after I was in my apartment that she was only a casual friend. However long she'd been in the picture, she was no longer a secret. I made it to all of Jess's events with a smile on my face. As usual, I did what I had to do. For almost a year, I grieved for everything. Joe, the only man I'd ever loved, was gone. It was over. But what was I going to do now?

We fell into a loose routine where Jessica spent most of her weeknights with me and stayed at her father's house on weekends. She eventually came around to accepting the new living situation. Where she studied and slept was only a small part of her busy life. She was enjoying every minute of her senior year. Sports, drama, studies, dances . . . and looking forward to college. My daughter's schedule was jam packed with activities and friends. She had a bright smile and a great attitude. Just being around someone so bursting with life and energy inspired me, when it wasn't filling me with regret about my own state of mind. Jessica reminded me of what I'd once been.

It took nearly a year of all-out wallowing, but as the holidays approached, I made a solemn vow to myself at Christmastime. Once again, enough was enough. It was time. This pity party was getting me exactly nowhere. I decided that I would pull myself together through sheer willpower. It started with a promise to myself to put down the wine, join a gym, and start coming to terms with the end of my marriage.

I found a gym, hired a personal trainer, and started working out. I had a lot of years left to live . . . what was I going to fill them with? I started haunting bookstores, leafing through all the various career change and business books. I resumed my volunteer work reading tapes for the blind. I liked to read, and I liked to talk, so it was a good fit for me. Slowly, fitfully, my confidence level and interest in life began to build. Certainly, I took two steps ahead then one step back. It wasn't the smoothest recovery in the world, but the daily gym trips helped. Getting strong physically reinforced my mental resolve, which thankfully started to return.

As the months passed, I became Joe's confidante, his pal, someone he could even complain to about his relationship with Evanka. We had started out as good friends in high school, after all, and I still cared about him. My birds were almost out of the nest. Paul lived an independent life in his own apartment on Joe's massive property. Jessica was in her last year of high school and planned to attend college in Santa Barbara after she graduated. There was no way I wanted to live in L.A. once Jessica was launched into the world, and I knew I couldn't return "home." Apart from the fact that I had come to love the California weather, Long Island was in the past. I couldn't return to any sort of life there. My family still lived there, sure, but that wasn't enough. Whether they were grown or not, I didn't want to live three thousand miles away from my kids. Also, I would always be a freak show in Massapequa. I would never again live the blissfully anonymous life I'd enjoyed for thirty-seven years. I had grieved the loss of that life for eight years now. It was time to move on, find acceptance, and build a new future. I needed to follow my daughter's example and learn to bloom where I was planted. I began to plan my next move, and Joe and I started discussing plans.

My sister, a pediatric occupational therapist, loved her job and found it very gratifying. I began to think this might be the right occupation for me, too. The first step would be to earn my associate's degree, and then go on to specialized schooling. In California, there were only three schools specializing in pediatric occupational therapy (OT) programs—the only one anywhere nearby was in Santa Ana, about ninety miles from my Woodland Hills apartment. I toured the school, liked what I saw, and made plans to begin all over again. It was a scary feeling, but I wanted to do it.

It was humbling to imagine going back to a life of homework assignments and tests. My only full-time job outside the home had been in the years following high school, in a bank, but that had in no way been a career. It was a job, to earn money while I lived with my parents, so Joe and I could buy a house and get married. The plan had always been that Joe would be the family breadwinner. I would raise the children and take care of the home. But here I was, children grown, alone in an apartment in California. It was time to figure out not only how I was going to earn a living, but what kind of job would really suit me, where my strengths lay, and whether or not I was good at anything besides caring for a family. School, I hoped, would provide some of these answers.

Joe didn't like this idea at all. "How about we rent you a little cottage in Santa Barbara. You can be near Jess and not so far away from us, too." He tried everything to manipulate me into this alternate plan, but I stuck to my guns. My being too independent wasn't part of his plan. I didn't want to go to Santa Barbara—pleasant as it sounded. I wanted Jessica to live her own life without me hovering, and I wanted to do what I needed to do without worrying about my kids. I found the most beautiful apartment in Newport Beach, a gorgeous seaside community just up the freeway from Santa Ana, and I knew I had found the perfect place for me.

As Joey and I were tussling over my future plans, notices started arriving in the mail at my apartment. Creditors were asking for money, and collection notices started showing up almost daily, coming after me for money owed by Joseph Buttafuoco. We were still legally married, after all. I learned that Joey had filed for bankruptcy six months earlier. (Of course, this was news to me until I confronted him). Unfortunately, his filing left me on the hook. Everyone came after me instead. That damn boat, the *Double Trouble* back on Long Island, is what precipitated this turn of events. He'd had to leave the boat there when we moved. Of course, we still had years of payments left on it. When he couldn't find a buyer, rather than continue to pay the loan company, Joe unilaterally decided to file for bankruptcy. Hey, no big deal, it was just filing some papers. He didn't care.

I was very alarmed when all the credit card notices started coming to me, and the phone rang all the time with dunning calls. "Just file for bankruptcy; it was nothing," was Joe's advice. I was furious. No matter what I did, this man dragged me down. I felt like I was climbing slowly and painfully out of a deep, dark hole, but had just gotten sucker punched again. I lived frugally. I didn't waste money. I cared deeply about my name and credit standing. A sociopath, on the other hand, has the same regard for financial obligations as he does to personal ones: no remorse, no conscience. Get what you want now, and damn the consequences later. When I got a clearer picture of how dire our debt situation really was, I realized he had left me no choice. I, personally, was going to have to file for bankruptcy, one of the most shaming acts of my life.

As I was getting all my papers together and awaiting my court date, some family back East flew out to California for Jessie's high school graduation. Our separation was well known by then. My sister stayed with me in my apartment. Joey's sister and her husband stayed with Joe in the big house. It was all very celebratory, family-oriented, and amicable. Evanka was nowhere to be seen. She vanished, at least for the weekend, as we put aside our personal issues to celebrate Jessica and her many accomplishments. Our daughter had been prom queen, was active in sports and the performing arts, and had a very bright future ahead. She deserved plenty of credit. I had no choice but to be around Joe and put on a happy face, but I was so angry that I could barely look at him. I was bracing myself for yet another legal matter that I had done nothing to cause but was forced to deal with.

Filing for bankruptcy was humiliating beyond belief, and trust me, I had known some humiliation in my life with Joe. I showed up at the crowded courtroom, a very public forum, with only my court-appointed lawyer for company, and waited for my name to be shouted out. I watched as the judge ran each person through a list of their creditors. "Can you pay this $2,033 charge to MasterCard?"

"No."

"Can you pay this $560 owed to the electric company?"

"No."

This process could go on for quite some time. I found it excruciatingly embarrassing. Finally, my name was called, and I approached the bench. We ran through the list of creditors and, just like everybody else, I had to answer "No" each time he asked if I could pay the bills. But I got a special set of questions. "Do you have any movie productions about your life in the works?" he asked.

"No," I answered.

"How about upcoming television shows or appearances?"

"No."

"Radio appearances?" This line of questioning went on and on. If no one had recognized me in the courtroom before, they were sure paying attention now. The judge wanted to be sure I had no plans to capitalize on my notoriety to make money. I had absolutely no plans for that. For one thing, the story was over. I had officially forgiven Amy, and she was free. Joey and I were separated. There was nothing about those days I wanted to revisit; I was doing my best to look forward.

The minute I completed the whole painful process, I got into my car and called Joe. I was beyond angry. I couldn't get my own apartment now because my credit would be in the toilet from this point on. Joey's credit was ruined, too, of course, but he could come up with cash, or charm the landlord, or do whatever it took. I grabbed the information about the new place in Newport Beach and dialed his number, even though we were barely speaking. "This is the address, this is the apartment number, these are the terms of the lease, and I don't care what it takes. You go down there and deal with it!"

"Okay, okay. Whatever you want, no problem . . ." We quickly reverted back into the exasperated mother/naughty son dynamic. He did whatever had to be done—fast—and I packed up my things and escaped to where I wanted to go for a change: Newport Beach.

I had grieved for our marriage for a year. Now anger kicked in with a vengeance. I decided that I was going to take Joe for everything I could from this point on. I would damn well live where I wanted in Newport Beach while I studied, with whatever furniture I wanted, too. "I need five thousand dollars for a new couch," I announced, and he handed over the money, no questions asked. Absolutely, I took advantage of his guilt over the fact that I was adrift in California, that he had a girlfriend, that he still wanted to control me—everything. I consciously decided to suck him dry—because I truly believed that's what he had done to me. Twenty-two years of my life—now it was my turn. Whatever he gave me, I more than deserved. That's what I told myself anyway.

I forced Joe to get me new credit cards, even though it was a big hassle because they had to be secured with cash due to our bankruptcies. "Okay, okay," he said meekly, and set about getting me new cards in my name. I was determined to rebuild my credit, though I had no way of earning my own money at the time. Whatever kept me quiet and happy was fine with him. I am not proud of my behavior and motivations at the time, but I certainly believed they were justified. And for the next eighteen months, I was happy. I really began to live again like I hadn't since I'd been shot.

CHAPTER 10

FLYING SOLO

I was now the proud resident of my own beautiful apartment decorated exactly the way I preferred with no husband or kids to mess it up! For the first time in my life, I could set something down, go out for a while, and find it just how I'd left it when I came home! I enrolled in community college, joined a local gym, and showed up faithfully every day at both places. I embarked on a strength-and-conditioning weight-training program, ran on the treadmill until I was exhausted, worked out hard on the elliptical machine, and even took an abs class. I was in the best shape of my life. I got very tan and even wore belly shirts! I had long ago come to terms with the injury that froze half my face. It looked a bit strange as I aged and my skin began its inevitable droop, but I didn't care. For the first time in years, I was comfortable in my own skin.

I had been so lonely in my first apartment, but now I relished my freedom. I used to come home from school sometimes and just stand in my doorway, gazing happily at my immaculate, quiet apartment. My job was complete: both my children were officially grown and living on their own. My heavy feelings of obligation and guilt over everything they'd endured throughout their fractured childhoods dissipated because it was over. I had done the very best I could in the very worst circumstances, and I was pleased and proud of the two young adults I had raised. Now I didn't have to solve anybody's problems, I didn't have to listen to anybody, and I didn't have to clean up after anybody for the first time in more than twenty-five years. I loved it.

Living in Newport Beach, a small coastal community, was the closest I'd felt to home for a long time. Being waterside with plenty of sun and visits to the beach all year round did a great deal to rejuvenate me. My heart and brain were healing more every month. Sometimes I'd take a leisurely drive up the coast—a gorgeous ride—to visit Jessica, who was thriving in Santa Barbara. I made a couple of casual new friends and occasionally went out to lunch or shopping with them. It was a time of personal growth, reflection, and healing.

I truly believed in my heart that I'd had my shot at love in this life. I'd married and had kids with the man I loved—and when it was over, it was over. Love was over for me. I had zero expectations of finding anyone else because there was no man out there who would be able to deal with my baggage—not my grown children, not the fact that I was divorced, not the bullet in my head, and especially not the big piece of Italian baggage named Joey Buttafuoco.

I was not much of a bar person. I went to the gym solely to

work out, and 90 percent of my classmates were the ages of my children. I didn't even bother looking for someone new because I had no idea where to look! Joe was not completely out of the picture. I still saw him occasionally. He and Evanka had a tumultuous relationship. They broke up and made up all the time, like teenagers. He was so familiar to me. He was all I knew, all I'd ever had. The pull was still strong, and occasionally I weakened and spent time with him.

We chatted on the phone a couple of times a week, and he always said all the right things: "I miss you, I love you, I want to see you . . . Why don't I come down this weekend? We'll hang out, have fun." We did have fun together. With the petty aggravations of day-to-day life with Joey gone, it was almost like we were dating again. My schedule was far from full. Wonderful and peaceful as it was to live alone, there were times I missed a male presence. I missed having sex, and Joey was always happy to oblige me there. I also had good reason to return to his house occasionally—to see Paul. Joey was always amenable to a visit from me. Every time I drove out the gates of that huge stone residence, I regretted my visit immediately and bitterly and got down on myself for a few days. Joey's spell was difficult to break. It was hard work to be strong. Two steps forward, one step back.

Whenever Joe really made me angry, I'd whip out a credit card and go shopping. Looking back, I'm ashamed of that behavior, but I had no other way of expressing my anger and feelings of subjugation. Blowing his money was the only way to get to him because it was all he ever cared about. It was the only way I had of expressing, *You really hurt me.* He had set up the game this way, and I played it. Whenever this happened, I'd get a phone call, and he'd laugh and say something like, "Boy, I must have pissed you off last week! Just got the bill from Pier One today!"

"Yeah, I was not happy!" I'd laugh, too, and he'd pay the bill and say no more about it. It was a very unhealthy dynamic, but one that we were both comfortable with. He enjoyed the power and sense of control that paying the bills gave him. I liked being on my own to sort out my life without the immediate pressure of making a living. Of course, I rationalized the situation to myself all the time: This man has caused all my problems. I have a bullet in my head because of him! I had to move to California because of him! He has cheated and lied and driven me crazy. If I want $500 worth of clothes, I'm getting them! It was my little fuck-you, the weapons of the weak, the only way I could stick it to him.

When I was thinking clearly and regretted this unhealthy behavior on my part, I'd speak more reasonably to him about money. "You've got a lot of big expenses going, Joe. How long can you keep this up?"

"Hey, no worries, everything's fine, no problem," he'd always say. Never a worry or a care. In other words, how he got his money was not my concern, so I didn't pry. Joe had always been a hard worker, an excellent provider, and as far as I knew, business at his auto body shop was booming. Joey had huge bills: a daughter in college, a girlfriend who demanded the best, a big house—I was the least of his expenses. As soon as I was out of the picture and living a safe distance away, he became increasingly reckless in his quest to make money: insurance scams, car repair fraud, renting out his house as a porn set, you name it.

I was blissfully unaware of the sordid details. Certainly Joe and Paul, who was exposed to far too many unsavory business deals and shady people, preferred to keep me in the dark. Joe wanted to remain in charge, do as he pleased, and not have to listen to me remonstrate. Paul just didn't want his mother to worry. I had a small sense of security knowing that I had taken out a huge life insurance policy on Joe years before, just in case something went wrong—as it inevitably did. I took Joe's advice and for once *didn't* worry. None of it was my business anymore anyway. The next two and a half years of my life were focused on coming to terms with being a single woman and figuring out what to do with the second half of my life.

～⁀ɔ

Obviously, I'd had plenty of physical therapy and people working on me during my recovery, which was a large part of why I was drawn to occupational therapy. To prepare for enrollment in the specialized OT program, I needed credits in algebra, English, and many other background courses. I had much preferred socializing to studying when I was young, so going back to school was a huge challenge for me. I had very little confidence in my academic abilities.

Joey and I weren't even legally separated, so I had enrolled in school as Mary Jo Buttafuoco. I was surrounded by kids, many of whom were too young to remember who I was, though certainly I got some looks in the halls from faculty and other adults. During my very first semester, I enrolled in a public speaking class. The first week, our instructor said, "We're all going to stand up, introduce ourselves, and tell each other a unique fact about ourselves; something nobody knows." My face started to burn. I had been so hoping to remain an anonymous student named Mary Jo.

When it was my turn, I stood up, faced the room, and said, "My name is Mary Jo Buttafuoco, and something unique about me is that I've been shot point-blank in the head." The whole room gasped. That was all; I sat back down. During that class, another middle-aged woman stated her name and said that she had survived a plane crash in New Jersey where two of the passengers had been killed. She sought me out after class, and we became friendly.

My English class was a joy. I loved to write and earned plenty of praise from my teacher. Algebra, on the other hand, was a real struggle. My brain just couldn't seem to grasp the concepts. The teacher, a lovely woman about my age, encouraged me and offered extra help and assistance. She even made me her teacher's aide. I certainly wasn't assisting in algebra instruction, but made copies, collected papers, and helped her any way I could. She was my cheerleader and assured me I was definitely going to get it. I started to believe in my heart that I really could become whatever I wanted to be. Baby steps, baby steps, but I was starting to make some solid progress.

But damned if Joey didn't still have a hold on me. Living in California, I had no network. I had no truly close friends in whom to confide. I continued to miss my family—my sisters, parents, Joey's huge extended family who I considered mine—who had all been such a big part of my life for decades. In California, it was just the four of us. Paul was an adult, and Jessica was busy at college. Besides, I would hardly confide in them about their father's and my relationship. I was still somewhat adrift. Even after all this time, it was strange to go from a town where I knew everyone and they knew me to the utter disconnectedness of life in California. It was very isolating and lonely, and I desperately wanted a confidante.

After nearly three years, by the spring of 2002, the novelty of "singlehood," a pristine apartment, and academic progress had worn off. I found myself feeling restless, a sort of "Is this all there is?" feeling. I was in a place where I was doing everything right for myself, for the right reasons, yet it wasn't as fulfilling as I'd hoped. Of course, sensing my ambivalence, Joe really turned up the heat. "I still love you. Come back. We could start all over again." My ego was gratified that he missed me. He pulled at all my heartstrings. "We've been married such a long time. We should try it again. We can make it work this time..." He was saying all the right things. We had never legally separated, and our relationship had been in limbo for quite some time.

It had still never even crossed my mind to start dating. I couldn't bear to imagine the first-date chat: *So, what do you do? Oh, that's nice. Want to hear what happened to me?* Even thinking about it made me weary. How would any man react when hearing that my husband and the father of my children was Joey Buttafuoco? I didn't even want to go there. I just took care of me. The conversations about us reconciling continued. The emotional pull was still strong, though the logical part of my mind kept saying, *Nothing's going to change.*

Not to mention that Joey had a serious girlfriend! "Listen, Joe, if we were ever to get back together, I'd have to be assured that Evanka is completely out of the picture and that you are finished with that woman," I told him.

"Oh, I am finished. It's done. She's gone . . . I want you back!" he assured me.

I went to stay for a couple of weekends at the house in Chatsworth, and Paul simply rolled his eyes at my appearance at the breakfast table. "What are you doing, Mom?" he asked. I was mystified by this attitude. "Why would you not want us to get back together?" I asked my son, but he refused to elaborate. "Oh, I don't know, never mind . . ." His loyalties were clearly divided. He didn't want to alienate his father, and he didn't want to hurt me, but he didn't want me back there. That much was clear.

I talked over the situation with an old friend of mine. Toni was on good terms with Joe, too, and she still liked him fine. I said to her, "You know, I've been thinking about going back to Joe."

"I think you should," Toni said. "You two are made for each other. He's a good provider. He still loves you . . . I think you should reconcile."

But in my heart of hearts, why would I believe he would change? I'd hoped and prayed a million times that he'd change and he hadn't—what made this any different? One night, I sat at home by myself and reviewed the whole history of Joe and me in my head—the great times, the horrible times, everything, as objectively as I could. And then I literally prayed: "Lord, if this marriage is meant to be, please show me the way. If this is what you want me to do, I'll do it. But I need a sign. Help me out here, please."

My girlfriend Blair from New York came to visit me for a weekend. We had a great time riding bikes along the beach and taking long walks on the pier, just hanging out. She had a steady boyfriend she'd been seeing for a couple of years. We talked about him for a while, and then the conversation turned to the topic of me dating.

"I'm forty-seven years old. Who's ever going to look at me? Sure, it would be nice to go on a date sometime, but no man has ever even looked in my direction," I told her.

Blair did a double take. "Are you kidding me? All kinds of men look at you, all the time! You just never look back!"

"Really?" I was surprised.

"Hey, I've been with you all weekend. I can see just fine. Guys are always checking you out, but you're oblivious! You put off that untouchable, unavailable vibe."

"What do you mean? Of course, I look at people . . ." But as I thought about it, I realized she might possibly have a valid point. I had felt like a hunted animal for so many years that it had become an unconscious habit to always keep my distance, put up an invisible shield around myself, and refuse to make eye contact with strangers. It was a simple, offhand remark, but it stayed with me long after Blair returned home. I took our conversation as the sign I had prayed for.

Maybe she's right. Maybe I don't ever look back. I decided to set a new goal. For the next few months, I was going to look people in the eye. I wasn't going to worry about being Mary Jo Buttafuoco. I was going to open myself up to the world again. If a nice man looked at me, I was going to look back.

Meanwhile, Joey was constantly on the phone with me, wheedling, calling, charming, asking me to give things another go, to come back and give our marriage one more try. Naturally, I was hesitating, knowing that nothing was going to change, but a certain weariness had set in. Maybe this was my destiny. Despite what Blair had said, I was pretty sure there was no one else out there in the world for me. Maybe Joey was my lot in life. Maybe there was a reason we had never divorced. I was still resisting his logic, albeit weakening.

Jessica was absolutely thrilled. "It would be wonderful if you got back together again!" She couldn't have been happier with the prospect. It's every child's dream, after all—to get Mommy and Daddy back together. Paul, on the other hand, looked at me once again like I was crazy. "Don't do it," he said flatly.

"Trust me, Mom, you don't want to come back. It's insane here. I can hardly stand it sometimes. You're doing so well—don't come back. Just stay away."

His attitude was really disturbing to me. I tried this time to pull more out of him, but Paul refused to get specific. "Evanka's still in the picture; I don't care what he's saying about that. And that's just for starters." Joe, of course, swore she was long gone.

I made a last-ditch effort in July 2002. My brother-in-law, a single man, was living at Joey's house and helping out at the auto body shop. I considered Bruce an older brother and wanted to spend some time with him. I decided to stay the weekend at the house in Chatsworth, and we all went out and had a nice, happy dinner. A Mexican restaurant, lots of margaritas ... it was pleasant and fun. We all got along very well, but something in me resisted. *I can't come back to this house. I can't, I can't ...*

"Whew," I said to my brother-in-law as we stumbled down for coffee late the next morning. "I need to get to the gym today and sweat out some of that tequila."

"I really should join you," Bruce mused. We agreed we would go, but we couldn't seem to get out the door. A couple of hours passed while we procrastinated. Joe, of course, was nowhere to be found. I even mentioned it to Bruce. "He's supposed to want me back so badly, so where is he? Why am I sitting around with you?" But, honestly, I didn't really care. He could have been at the shop, but more likely he was with Evanka, and his absence wasn't breaking my heart. That realization led me to admit that I was not committed to coming back.

Bruce and I finally got into our gym clothes and into the car. On the way, our regular route was closed; the whole street was blocked off. We looked over to see what was going on and noticed a classic car show. Gorgeous hot rods and bands and classic cars were all over the place. It was a huge street fair.

As a woman who was immersed in the auto body business for many years, I couldn't resist this. The depressed, pity-party Mary Jo would have just gone home, but I said to Bruce, "Come on, let's stop by and see what's going on." We wandered in, and the first person I saw was George Barris, king of custom-made cars, the man who created the Monkee Mobile, the Munster Mobile, and so many others. As we headed over to George's booth, Bruce and I both recognized a guy working the booth who used to work as a pinstriper at Complete Auto Body back on Long Island. His name was Tommy.

We were all quite surprised to see each other and had a nice little reunion, talking about old times. Bruce and I stood in the booth for quite a while, catching up as groups of people came and went, meeting and getting autographs from George. I noticed a good-looking man about my age who had been standing nearby for a while, glancing over at me every now and then. Blair's words rang in my mind. I decided to look back. I looked him straight in the eye and smiled at him—and he smiled back and came over.

The man introduced himself as a friend of Tommy's, and

soon enough I found myself actually flirting. Tony was just my type: Italian, with a muscle shirt on, a motorcycle owner, big, strong, and macho. I was really having fun, a fantastic time actually, when I glanced up and saw Joe approaching. Boy, did I not want him to be there—not on the first occasion I had flirted with another man since high school!

Joey arrived and brought me back to earth with a thud. Now that Mr. Life of the Party was here, he took over all the attention and dominated the conversation. I faded into the background as usual. I stood there and thought, *I'm not going back. I'm not a second-class citizen. If I go back, all this forward motion will have been for nothing. I'm not going to live in his shadow ever again. I don't care if I'm alone for the rest of my life, so be it. Even if I am lonely sometimes, I'd rather be by myself.*

Bruce, Joey, and I all left the show together, and I realized there was really nothing at that house for me. The rest of the weekend passed uneventfully, but I was not feeling much at all. No love, no desire, certainly not wanting to ever come back to that house. I drove back to my apartment in Newport and thought about things. Okay, there was nothing left at Joey's house for me. What else was out there? For a few nights, I studied my old friend Tommy's business card. Finally, I decided to put myself out there. I called Tommy to ask him about his friend. Maybe he'd be married with five kids. I had no idea, but I was going to find out.

"What's the deal with your friend Tony?" I asked him casually, after some pleasantries about how nice it had been to catch up and so on.

"Oh, he's a great guy. He works with George Barris. I've known him a long time. He has a little boy, but he's not married." My heart did a tiny little leap upward. Tommy told me that George was appearing at a big custom car show in Las Vegas in a couple of weeks with a huge display. Tony would be there working, of course. The wheels in my head started turning. *I should show up and run into this guy Tony,* I thought.

"That sounds like a lot of fun," I said.

"Oh, we're all going to be there. It's going to be great!" Tommy went on and on.

"You know, I was thinking of going to Vegas myself in a couple of weeks," I said casually. "Could you do me a favor, Tommy? Could you call Tony and just find out if he'll definitely be there? He was really nice. Maybe I'll stop by and say hi." I could not believe what I was doing. I hadn't done anything like this in thirty years! But I was happy, it was fun, and I was excited for the first time in a long time.

A couple of days passed, and the phone rang with an unknown number. And just as I am wary of answering doorbells, unidentified numbers prompt me to screen the call. When I listened to the voice mail, it was Tony! The message said, "Hi, Mary Jo. Tommy gave me your number. It was great to meet you at the show . . ." My heart was pounding like a sixteen-year-old girl. *He called me! He called me!* My mouth was dry, and I paced around excitedly . . . It was unbelievable to me that I could feel and act this way again. *He called! Should I call him back? What do I say? What should I talk about? Does he know who I am?*

I didn't know the "rules" of dating, so I didn't wait three days to call Tony back. I called him back that night and acted very casual, though I was falling apart inside. I'm telling you, I was a teenager. We stayed on the phone for half an hour and had a very pleasant conversation about cars, old friends, and his son. We stayed completely off the subject of Joe. It was going so well that I was really emboldened. "Hey, I'll be meeting a friend in Vegas that weekend," I totally lied. "I'd love to stop by and hang out at the car show."

"That would be nice," he said. I was putting myself out there in a big way, but it seemed to be working all right.

The week before the show, Joey called me. The power had shifted, and I was now putting him off. "I really love you. I want you to come back . . ." Not so fast! The timing was suddenly very inconvenient. I said, "You know, Joe, I want to stay here in Newport through January to get the school credits I need. It's not a good time for me to leave right now. I'm making great progress. Tell you what, let's see how everything goes, and we'll think about me coming home for Christmas."

This discussion bought me about six months. I decided to give the single life until the end of the year to see what unfolded and make a decision then. Maybe I really was destined to live out my days with Joe. But, meanwhile, I was very distracted. And he could sense it. "Remember when we saw Barris at that car show?" he suddenly asked.

"Oh, sure," I said cautiously.

"Yeah, I got a call from Tommy. Heard you really hit it off

with Tony," he said. Oh boy, apparently word traveled fast. It felt like we were back in high school.

I left that one alone. "It was good to see those guys again," or something like that was all I could say.

"So . . . you know that big car show in Vegas coming up? It got postponed. George couldn't get the right permits for Vegas in time, ya know," Joe said.

"Really?" I asked. What bad luck for me.

"Yeah, I was talking to Tommy and George, and apparently there was a problem." I felt like a deflated balloon, but I wasn't about to discuss the matter any further. We hung up, and I felt very sad. The old me took every word Joey said as gospel. The new me decided to call Tony and ask about the change of plans. It gave me a good excuse to call him, if nothing else.

He was happy to hear from me, and we were having a pleasant chat when I said offhandedly, "I was talking to Joey and he mentioned that the car show in Vegas was canceled . . . that's too bad."

"That's news to me. I plan on being there next week," Tony said.

"You sure there was no problem with the permits?" I asked.

"I don't know what you're talking about. I mean, I can ask George, but there's no problem with permits. That's crazy. Of course we're going—we go every year. It's the biggest car convention in the country!"

The controlling and bullshitting on Joey's part was never going to stop. If I'd had any doubts before, they were banished.

I was for sure going to Vegas. And I wasn't going to tell anyone I was going or say another word about it. Tony and I met for a friendly lunch before that weekend, and we had a nice little vibe going. He took me to visit his shop, where I was reintroduced to George and saw all the amazing cars on which they were hard at work. It was great to be out again. I had to admit that putting myself out there was getting great results so far.

I had no problem imagining myself driving to Vegas and walking into that car show to see Tony again. The flirtatious girl I'd been thirty years ago in high school came back with a vengeance. A surge of confidence came over me. I was going to give it a try! This behavior was so uncharacteristic of me, yet it was the "me" I remembered from so many years ago. I was nervous, afraid, and seriously out of practice, but I was going to do it. I was going to try because my girlfriend said that I never looked back. I was a good person. I deserved to have some fun, and I was going to look back. Who knew that deciding to look back would be the first step in moving forward?

The morning I set off for Las Vegas, I was singing all the way. It was so thrilling to have someone who took my mind off Joe for a change. Someone in Vegas was waiting to see me! Not Joe's wife, nor the sidekick, the drag, or the wet blanket. It was so cute—Tony called me twice while I was driving. "Where are you? When are you getting here?" I was driving, but I felt like I was flying. I hadn't felt this happy and excited in years. I had forgotten I was capable of feeling this elated.

I checked into my room at the Rio Hotel, a place I'd been

many times before with Mr. Good Times Joey, but he was the last thing on my mind. I took a taxi across the street over to the Palms, where the show was being held. It was less than a mile away, but it was the middle of August and probably 120 degrees in the desert.

Tony was genuinely happy to see me when I arrived at his booth. He greeted me with a big hug and kiss, and I felt much better—not so much like a wanton woman chasing after some guy. He was thrilled that I was there. I was thrilled, too—and scared. I hadn't dated in more than thirty years. The excited part battled with the nervous part, especially as the day wore on and I foresaw myself being alone with Tony. I wanted my big brother around, someone to look after me a bit, help me if I needed it. Joe's brother Bruce was truly that figure in my life. I loved him as much as my own sisters.

I called him from the show and told him how amazing the displays were and what a great time I was having. He decided to jump on the thirty-minute flight and come see the show. I knew Joey, of course, would get wind of this plan, as Bruce lived in his house and would tell him where he was headed. I also knew that Joe's pride wouldn't allow him to react negatively. Plus, he had his hands full with a serious girlfriend. Whatever he really might be feeling about my weekend wasn't my concern. I felt like the forty-seven-year-old virgin and simply wanted a friend by my side. I was excited and scared to death at the same time.

After the show ended for the day, Tony, Bruce, and I had a lovely dinner with George Barris, where I met some very fancy-shmancy bigwigs from the car industry and a few celebrities. I was having a great time, one thing led to another, and I soon had a decision to make. I was a forty-seven-year-old woman who had slept with one man her entire life. It was a big leap to consider actually becoming intimate with someone else. But I thought about my girlfriend, Toni, who'd had many boyfriends over the course of her life. "You've seen one, you've seen 'em all," she used to say. I wasn't in love with Tony. I was giddy with excitement, fun, and anticipation. I was saying *yes* for a change. To everything!

Bruce stayed in my room because I didn't use it that night. I lay awake all night long while Tony slept peacefully. I could not believe I had done this! It was a momentous event. The butterflies and the high from this entire night would not allow me to rest for even one hour. When Tony woke up, he couldn't have been nicer, but I urged him to go ahead to the show without me. I would find breakfast and meet him later. I was exhausted, but still too wound up to sleep. I raced around like a teenager, running on sheer nerves, and prepared for the day.

I was having such a good time with Tony that I spent the entire day hanging out in the booth. I didn't want to leave his side, even to go gamble. I was wearing a cute little pair of shorts and a matching tank top and feeling great. At one point, Tony got a call on his cell phone and told me when he hung up, "Hey, that was my friend Stu; he's here in town. He's staying at the Rio, too, so I told him to come by and say hi. You'll like him. He's from Long Island, too—Bellmore."

I had been absolutely reveling in a feeling of anonymity all weekend. I wasn't Joey's wife, he was nowhere around, and I didn't know or care if anyone was aware of my history. For the past two days, I had simply been "Mary Jo," and I liked it that way. My heart sank a bit. Anyone from Long Island would certainly know who I was, but I put it out of my mind.

A couple of hours later, a man about our age showed up and found Tony. I was standing in a fast-food place inside the casino, munching on some French fries, not paying much attention to who was coming and going, when Tony motioned me over. "Mary Jo, come over here . . . This is my friend Stu I was telling you about." He had just walked a mile across the street in the blazing midday desert sun and was sweating and out of breath.

"Hi Stu," I said, "so nice to meet you."

"Nice to meet you, too," he replied.

"So, you're from Long Island, too," I said.

"Yep, that's right," Stu said.

"Well, I guess you know who I am," I said, half cringing, waiting for the inevitable.

"No . . . who the fuck are you?" he answered abruptly. Clearly, he was a little out of sorts. I was so embarrassed, my face burned. I didn't know what to say.

"Sorry, I thought you said you were from Long Island!" I said.

"Well, yeah, but I left in 1979," he said. I glared at Tony. He hadn't mentioned that part. Now Stu was really looking at me closely. "So who *are* you?"

"Never mind, never mind, forget it," I said, wishing I could just fade away. In fact, that's what I did—I just walked away, leaving a very puzzled Stu behind me. "Am I supposed to know who she is or something?" he was asking Tony as I got out of there—fast. Hardly a storybook beginning! I could not have imagined that this man would soon become the love of my life.

My Eighth Grade Graduation from
St. Rose of Lima in Massapequa, 1970.

Joey's and my engagement party, May 1977.

Our wedding day, September 4, 1977. I couldn't have been
a happier bride. I knew this was the right thing to do.

At my parent's house during the throes of Joey's addiction, 1986.

The lights of my life—
our son, Paul, and daughter, Jessica, 1988.

New Year's Eve 1990. Joey was sober, and I thought that everything I worked so hard for had finally come together.

On Christmas 1991, I was perfectly content. I had no idea the sociopath I lived with was finding life just a little bit too dull.

May 17, 1992, two days before I was shot and two days
after my 37th birthday. We were going to a friend's daughter's
communion party on the North Shore of Long Island.
It was a perfect day that I thought was going
to be the start of a perfect summer.

Around noon on Tuesday, May 19, 1992. This is the bench I was painting when I was interrupted by the doorbell ringing.

These are the gloves I was wearing and holding in my hand when Amy shot me.
The dark spots are blood.

The jacket I was wearing.

What's left of the T-shirt I had on—
paramedics had to cut it off of me.

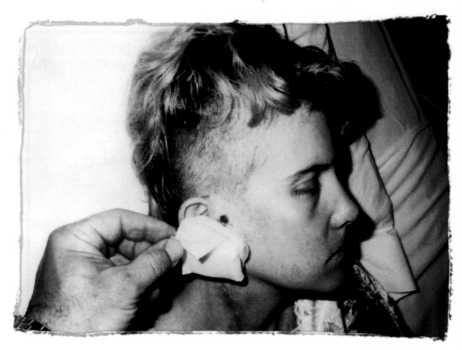

In the hospital—the bullet hole had to be cleaned out and packed four times a day. It was agony.

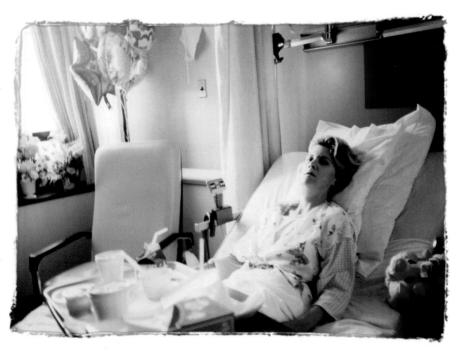

Surrounded by flowers, balloons, and Jessica's favorite stuffed animal pig, I still couldn't believe what was happening.

A view from my bedroom window. The media was a constant, intrusive presence in our once quiet neighborhood.

The Board at the Biltmore Beach Club voted to put a gate in our backyard so we didn't have to go out the front door. The beach club and our friends and family were the only respite we had that summer of 1992.

A home-made get well card from my daughter, Jessica.

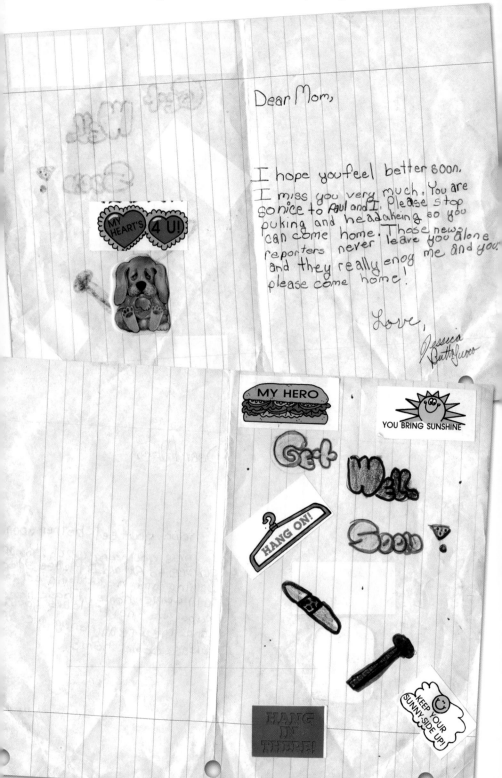

Dear Mom,

I hope you feel better soon. I miss you very much. You are so nice to Paul and I. Please stop puking and headaheing so you can come home. Those news reporters never leave you alone and they really enog me and you. please come home!

Love,
Jessica
Battafuoco

MY
HEART'S 4 U!

MY HERO

YOU BRING SUNSHINE

Get

Well

Soon!

HANG ON!

HANG IN THERE!

KEEP YOUR SUNNY-SIDE UP!

September 1992. My first TV interview from my home.
Raphael Abromowitz, a reporter for the news magazine
Hard Copy, and crew in my living room.

Thanksgiving 1992. Thanksgiving had a very special meaning
to our families that year and Joey's and
my family celebrated it together.

At my sister Eileen's wedding, April 22, 1994.
I was hoping that life was returning to some sort of
normalcy, but a month later Joey was arrested for soliciting
a hooker in L.A., starting the insanity all over again.

Standing in front
of our rental house
in Agoura Hills,
California, feeling
very alone in the
winter of 1997.

Paul's high school graduation, 1998.

Jessica's high school graduation, June 2001.
It's funny, looking at this picture now, we had been
separated for a year and a half by then, and yet I still
leaned into him when our picture was being taken.

The Buttafuoco family: Joey and his brothers and sisters. From left to right: Joey, Bobby, Bruce, Anne, and Lucretia.

The Connery family: My sisters, parents, and me at my parents' house in Maine, August 2002. Left to right top: me, Ellen, my mom Pat, Kathy, and Jeanne. Dad, Al, in middle and Eileen in front.

My new life! Stu and me in
our backyard, June 2008.

Stu and me in 2008
before a friend's
wedding.

"Our" kids—from left to right (back row): Martine, Paul, and Jessica; (front): C.J. and Hutton.

CHAPTER 11

LOVE REDUX

I was having the time of my life mingling in the huge anonymous crowds at the car show in Las Vegas. Tony hadn't mentioned my history to anyone the entire weekend. We had just been two people hanging out, having fun with all kinds of other car buffs. Tony had met Joe and Bruce at the fair in the Valley. He and I had talked a bit about my marital situation, but that was all. He had no interest in hearing about Amy Fisher, my injury, or Joey. Years of being pointed at and whispered about had taken their toll. I was constantly paranoid that everyone had heard of me and recognized me. To Tony, I was simply Mary Jo, a nice woman who had accompanied him to the show, which felt freeing.

When Tony explained my rather unique situation to his old friend Stu—and mentioned my last name for the first time—Stu was mortified that he'd spoken so sharply to me. When I showed up at the booth an hour or so later, Stu walked right up to me.

"I am so sorry. You must think I am the rudest idiot. I had just walked a mile from the Rio—it's 120 degrees outside—and I hate the heat. Maybe you can tell by the looks of me that I'm not a big walker," he said, as he gestured toward his husky stature. "I can't tell you how sorry I am." Clearly, he felt terrible, but I just laughed it off. It was a very minor incident. I was so caught up in Tony and the excitement of a new man, what did I care? I didn't give it, or Stu, another thought.

On my drive home on Sunday I was on cloud nine. When I thought of Joey, I knew there was no way I was ever going back. There were other possibilities in the world. I had found a nice guy who liked me and didn't care who I'd been married to. Tony and I began dating. He introduced me to his circle of friends, who were the most fun, warm people I'd met since I moved to California. Several were married couples, and there were a few singles. All of them were friendly, down-to-earth men and women who couldn't have cared less that my last name was Buttafuoco. Together we had great times, and I could not have been happier.

A few weeks into the relationship, Jessica accompanied me on a trip back East for a long-planned family reunion. My daughter was pleased to see me looking so good, laughing, joking, and glowing. Much as she would have liked her parents to reconcile, she could see that I was blossoming. Whatever I was doing, or whoever I was seeing, was clearly good for me.

For forty-plus years I had played by the rules. I had done everything a good Catholic girl, wife, and mother was supposed to do. I remained very dependent on my parents' approval. For the first time, as I spent time with them at the reunion, I decided to reevaluate this relationship, too. Dating Tony had done wonders for my confidence. I decided I was going to live how I wanted for a change, and if they didn't approve, so be it.

My father and I sat outside, just the two of us, and I poured out my heart to him. "Dad, I've been so unhappy, so lonely. It's not going to work out with Joe. We were talking about getting back together, but I can't do it. I've met a man, and he's really great. I feel like I'm a teenager again. He makes me happy."

"Mary Jo," my father said, "turn the page. It's your life, and you need to live it. Turn the page and start a new chapter." It was amazing that my father, of all people, would say this to me. My mother, bless her heart, took a much harder line when she heard that I, technically still a married woman, was dating someone new.

"Well, do what you want, Mary Jo, but you're going to have to answer to God," she said, sighing.

"You know what, Mom? I certainly hope so, because I've got a few questions I'd really like to ask him!" I replied. My sisters broke out laughing; even my father had to chuckle. I wouldn't have dreamed of speaking like this ever before in my life, but at nearly fifty years old I was becoming my own person. It was high time. Another layer of the onion peeled off. I realized once and for all that I wasn't going back to Joe. It wasn't because Tony was the be-all and end-all of my life—we had just started to see each other—but because there were all kinds of possibilities out there, whether I was alone or with someone else.

I couldn't behave like Joey and hide who I was seeing and what I was doing. Even though we were separated, my conscience bothered me. I decided the right thing to do was to tell Joe about Tony. I got on the phone that night from Maine and said, "Look, Joe, I met a nice man and I'm dating him. I'd like to see what happens, so obviously now's just not the time to reconcile."

I can't even remember what he answered. Whatever it was, I didn't care and hung up quickly. His opinion no longer concerned me. I was in a real zone, especially after the discussion with my mother. I had spoken up, and the world had continued turning. All my life I had worried about standing up for myself around my mother, but it had turned out fine. I absolutely believed that God sent an angel named Tony to show me my self-worth and plant the idea that there were other men in the world I might be happy with. I felt strong and empowered for the next day or so at the reunion. From Maine, Jessica and I drove down to New York the night before we flew home. We had such a fun girls' night out. It was absolutely wonderful, the perfect end to a very satisfying trip.

Jessie and I returned to our hotel room late that night. I was in the bathroom washing my face when I suddenly heard her wail, "What? No! How could you do that?!" She sounded absolutely distraught. I shut off the water and stuck my head out of the door.

Jessie was on her cell phone, tears literally rolling down her face. "What's the matter?" I asked.

She threw down the phone and said, "She moved back in! Evanka's back! He knows how much we hate her, and Daddy moved her back in because you told him you weren't coming back!" Jessica was absolutely beside herself. "I'm not going back there. I'm not!"

I got on the phone. "What are you saying to her, Joe? For God's sake, I didn't say I was going to marry the guy. We've been on a few dates! What are you doing?" It had been literally twenty-four hours since we'd last spoken! I tried to console Jessica, but she wasn't having any of it. The last night of our trip was ruined.

When our plane landed in California the next evening, Jessica absolutely refused to go back to her father's house in Chatsworth. She insisted on returning to Santa Barbara. It was summertime, before classes began again, but she would not go to the house if Evanka was there. She preferred to find something—anything—to do in Santa Barbara. She was an adult, so I let her go and went back to Newport with a heavy heart.

I was hardly looking to get married again, but I was giddy with the excitement of a new relationship and the fun of dating. Tony, however, was the eternal bachelor. No one had ever tied him down before, and he wasn't about to make an exception for me. At fifty years old, he'd never even had a steady girlfriend!

He'd meet a woman, conquer her, then quickly move on to the next. He was very charming and managed to stay friendly with his ex-girlfriends. At the time we were dating, I wasn't aware of his extensive dating history. All I knew was that he started to pull away after a few weeks, once the infatuation had faded.

Tony had many of Joe's qualities. He liked to push the envelope, take risks, and above all have a good time, always. He was a real macho man. It was clear to me that this was not what I needed in my life on a permanent basis, even if he had been more emotionally available. It was all fun and games and laughs with Tony, and I'd had plenty of those already. It was pretty obvious that we weren't meant to be—to both of us. But I was in no hurry to give up the pleasure of a romance again.

"So, what are we going to do this weekend?" I asked him one night on the phone.

"I've got errands to run this weekend, so I don't really have time to get together," Tony said. He was backing off, and my feelings were hurt. This guy most definitely did not want to be one-half of a couple. It wasn't love, and had never been love, but we both got a little testy as the relationship wound down. We'd had such fun together—going out dancing, to concerts, out for sushi, hosting cookouts. Tony's circle was the best group of friends I'd made since leaving Long Island. Stu was in this group and was someone I enjoyed chatting. He was a funny guy. I liked him a lot—I liked all of them a lot. I regretted the prospect of losing them as much as I regretted losing Tony. I would miss their company.

Joe called one night, as he did periodically, and asked about Tony. "Things didn't really work out," I told him.

"Oh, I wish you had told me sooner!" Joe said.

"No one told you to move Evanka back in literally two minutes after I mentioned that I was going on a few dates!" I was tired of his nonsense. I didn't care who lived where. The breathtaking speed with which he'd gotten Evanka back was the last straw—if she'd ever really been gone. I needed to enjoy my life without Joey in it. Whether that meant dating again, or if Tony had been my one and only final fling in this life, that was fine with me. I was going to live without interference from Joey from here on out. "I" had come back. I was reclaiming the "me" I'd been before marrying Joe, having kids, and Amy Fisher. The hold Joe had on me, by virtue of thirty years spent together if nothing else, was finally, *finally* loosening and slipping off for good.

～

Stu called me one night. "So, will you be at the bar this Friday night?"

"I don't think so, Stu. Tony and I aren't really dating anymore . . ."

"Come on—listen, that's just Tony. He'll never stick with anybody for long. Believe me, I've known him for twenty years. He's never going to change. Why don't you come by anyway? I'd love to see you. In fact, I'd really like to take you out!"

I had to laugh. "Oh, great, just pass me around like a bag of chips!"

"It's not like that . . . really. Mary Jo, I'd love to take you out. Just stop by. All of us will be there. Please come," Stu said.

My new attitude said, *Why not? Why not, indeed?* I liked all of these people, and they liked me. Stu was inviting me to come by, so why the hell not? It was one night of my life.

I was fully aware that the situation was somewhat awkward. When I walked into Residuals, a popular bar/nightspot in the Valley that night, Tony did not look pleased to see me. Stu, on the other hand, was beaming. We all sat there awkwardly for a minute, and then I turned to Brett, the other single man in the group, and said, "When I'm done with Stu, you're next. After that, I'm going after Rick. I plan to work my way through all of you!" Everyone burst out laughing, and the tension immediately vanished. We all had a great time that night, and Stu was clearly smitten with me. This was his big chance, but to me, it was a casual night out with friends. As the night wore on, it became obvious that this man really, really liked me. He bought my drinks, touched me when he spoke, laughed at all my jokes, and walked me to my car when it was finally time to call it a night.

I liked him, too, but more than that, I loved my newfound freedom. That short-lived fling with Tony had done absolute wonders for me, even though it was clearly over. *I can do this,* I thought. *I can date. I can get out in the world and have a good time!* It wasn't that I wanted another boyfriend, but I was intoxicated by the possibilities. I had played by the rules all my life. I wasn't doing anything wrong or bad. If I wanted to go out and play the field a bit, who cared? I was going to have a good time. Stu, meanwhile, began to call me frequently. We forged a much deeper friendship during many late-night chats, some lasting as long as four hours. It was good to have a confidante, and I enjoyed his conversation very much. He could be a bit abrupt sometimes, as I'd seen the day I met him, but underneath he was a very kind man.

Stu owned a printing business in Chatsworth—oddly enough, just a mile from Joe's auto body shop. In a city as spread out as L.A., what were the chances of that? I lived eighty miles away in Newport Beach. We spent so much time on the phone that I really came to know him in a way I might not have face-to-face. It turned out that Stu had also been through quite a lot of drama, including infidelity and drug abuse, with both his former wives. He had pretty much sworn off relationships when I came along. He was a devoted weekend father to his young son, C.J., and daughter, Hutton. Martine, who was sixteen, spent less time with him because she was busier with friends and high school. All three children lived with their mothers.

One night on the phone, Stu began talking about Martine, who had lived with her mother since she and Stu split up when she was only a baby. He told me of the deep sorrow he felt over missing so much of her life. Now she was a moody teenager, involved with her own social life, and soon would be completely grown. He bitterly regretted all the milestones in her life he had missed and worried that it was too late to ever catch up.

"I can't believe I'm telling you this," he said suddenly. "I've never talked to anyone about how I feel about the situation with Martine." He was opening his heart to me, and I sympathized.

"I never would have imagined I'd be a middle-aged guy, divorced twice, with three kids by two different mothers," Stu mused. "You get married, you stay married, you work things out . . . that's always what I believed. I still believe it! I'm not a cheater. I love my children and want to spend time with them. I always provided . . . I just married women who wanted something more. Regular married life was too boring for them. They needed *excitement* all the time."

Oh, could I ever relate to *that*.

John Walsh had a new show on the air—a regular talk show this time, not *America's Most Wanted*. One of his producers called me out of the blue and asked if I would come to New York to appear on a show about regular people who had become overnight tabloid sensations. The other guest was going to be Kim Goldman, sister of Ronald Goldman, who had been murdered alongside Nicole Simpson. Kim was a young woman who I very much wanted to meet. I also admired John Walsh and all the good he'd done for others, so I accepted the invitation. I stayed with Joey's sister, Anne, and her husband, Ken. Of course, I filled Anne in on what was going on in my life and told her that I was seeing a nice man, but it was nothing serious.

"Oh, but you and Joey are fated to be together," she said with great assurance. "It's destiny. You two are meant to be . . . I hope it will happen soon."

"I don't know, Anne . . ." was all I could say. I didn't want to crush her hopes, but I knew there was no going back.

Stu and I had become quite close over the phone. Off the phone, we had what I considered a pleasant dating relationship, but nothing more. For one thing, it was hard for the two of us to spend any real quality time together. There was always an event with the kids, or a last-minute rush print job, and eighty miles was a real obstacle given Southern California traffic.

After a couple of months of casual dating, Stu suggested we go on vacation to Las Vegas for a nine-day getaway. I had grown very fond of Stu, but this sounded like a little too much togetherness to me. I didn't want to live with anyone again, and nine straight days in a hotel room was definitely living with someone. But again, I gave myself a lecture about being more open. *Just do it!* I told myself. Vegas was only a four-hour drive away from my apartment. If things didn't work out, I was free to leave whenever I wanted. I could do what I wanted; we weren't married. I should try to enjoy some time off with this very sweet man, I told myself, and go with a good attitude and an open mind.

And, lo and behold, from the moment we arrived, I felt perfectly at ease with Stu. Everything just seemed right. We had a great time together, and none of it was too much. Far from feeling crowded, I wanted only to stay by his side. As the days passed, I shared my most private feelings and fears with him—about everything—and he did the same. We had similar values. He not only listened, but he understood and empathized with everything I was saying. I felt open and vulnerable—in a good way. The most amazing feeling of love, acceptance, and warmth radiated from Stu. I felt both comforted and comfortable. We laughed, went shopping, had drinks, ate great meals, saw shows, and spent lots of quiet time together talking seriously, and I loved every minute of it.

All my life, I had been drawn to big, dark Italian men. Stu didn't fit my physical type at all—in any way. When I was a young and shallow girl, I wouldn't have given Stu a second look. But my eyes opened in Las Vegas. All of a sudden, I realized he had the most beautiful eyes—and a wonderful smile. While we were gambling, it struck me that he had such nice hands. And so on and so on. I couldn't believe I hadn't noticed it before—Stu was such a good-looking man! In fact, I couldn't take my eyes off him. What can I say? The chemistry kicked in! I was in love! Much to my surprise, nine solid days joined at the hip wasn't enough. When the vacation ended—much too soon—and I was back in my apartment in Newport, I was lonely. I missed Stu. I wanted to be with him all the time. I started living for the weekends.

Stu's daughter Hutton was seven, and his son C.J. was eleven. Both were exceptionally beautiful children, and they seemed to take to me immediately. They were good kids, and

I truly liked them and enjoyed the time we spent together every other weekend. Martine, who lived with her mother, had her own car, so we didn't see too much of her. She had boy-friends and lots of teenage dramas. My heart was wide open. I treated all three of them exactly as I would my own kids, even though I wasn't raising them.

I met Stu's brother and his wife, and his mother Thelma, all of whom immediately welcomed and loved me. The secure feeling of being part of a big family returned, and it made me more content and grounded than I'd been in years. I'd had a gaping hole in my life for so long due to the loss of my huge, ex-tended family in Long Island, and now I was being taken in by a new family who eagerly embraced me. They were happy be-cause Stu was happy, but more than that, they cared about me personally and showed it. I liked it. I liked everything about Stu—and so did my children.

Joey, of course, was still a part of my life. I supposed he al-ways would be, and that was my biggest fear as I adjusted to an entirely new kind of relationship with Stu. What impressed me was how well Stu dealt with it all. He wasn't threatened or intimidated by Joe. He let it all roll off his back. It dawned on me that all my life I had been defining the ideal of a "man" based on physical strength and a certain macho quality—the big guy who could roll into a party with a keg on his shoulder. I was so wrong. Stu's unconditional love and acceptance demonstrated in every gesture what a real man was. Stu showed by example a different kind of man to my son Paul. He was hardworking, honest, straightforward, and dependable. Before long, both of my kids came to love him as much as I did. Joe, of course, was well aware of the unfolding situation. One day, a couple of months into our relationship, Stu called me in a minor panic. "I just got a phone call from Joey. He's on his way over here to talk to me. . . . Do I need to worry?"

"Naaahhhh, you'll be fine, you'll see," I said. Stu, of course, only knew Joe from television and the many, many stories he'd heard. He had reason to be apprehensive, of course, but I knew that Joe would turn on the charm. To ease the tension, Paul accompanied his father on his visit.

Stu called me as soon as they left, half-relieved, half-bemused. "He was great," Stu said. "I thought he was going to break both my arms, but he shook my hand and told me what a wonderful woman you have always been and still are. His advice was never to leave you alone on May 19, and he reminded me your favorite color was pink. He had nothing but wonderful things to say about you."

I wasn't surprised. Joe really could be the most affable, charming guy. Plus, he had been involved with Evanka for quite some time. There was no reason for jealousy or threats. Even though just a few short months ago he'd been begging me to return, he had certainly adjusted quickly to the new situation—in about an hour, I would say. He was his old breezy nice-guy/great-neighbor self.

My gorgeous waterfront place, my privacy, my freedom to do what I liked—I still enjoyed them all, but I wanted to be with Stu. He had his business in Chatsworth, and his children lived nearby. If one of us had to relocate, I was much freer to move. I lay awake for hours at night, thinking. I had worked hard to grow into the best possible version of "me" while coming to terms with living alone, possibly for the rest of my life. I'd also set some ambitious goals at school. Given all I'd been through, I was the very last person in the world to advocate that a man was the answer to any woman's life.

Still, love had miraculously found me—something I never believed could happen—and it would be foolish, at the age of forty-eight, to let this opportunity slip away or waste precious time on a long-distance relationship, waiting to see what *might* happen. Something great had already happened! Within three months of our trip to Vegas, I finished my classes, withdrew from school, and gave up my place. Paul packed up all my things, and I moved into Stu's apartment in Los Angeles. Technically, I was still married to Joe. In reality, our marriage had been over for a long time, but the time had definitely come to officially make the break.

Joe had been happy enough being married to me and keeping secrets, being separated from me and openly seeing other women while keeping me in the picture, or juggling any kind of arrangement, actually. Legalities weren't a big deal to him, obviously. I wasn't like that. I couldn't possibly live with one man while I was married to another. I filed for divorce in

Ventura County and picked up the papers at the courthouse. I drove them to Joe's office myself, where I handed them to Paul. The legal rules state that a third person must serve divorce papers to the recipient, so Paul took them from me and handed them to his father.

It was a bittersweet moment, but certainly one that was inevitable. We did our best to make light of the situation, but the finality of the moment was sad. The end of any long marriage is always sad—even one like mine. The children were grown, so they weren't an issue. We amicably hashed out a very reasonable support agreement. The decree became final a few months later. The New York papers picked up the story—a few "What took her so long?" kind of articles appeared. Our twenty-five-year marriage had run out of steam and sputtered to this anticlimactic ending in the back office of an auto body shop in California. It was officially over. Except, of course, with Joey it's never really over.

Given all of the medical trauma in my life, it was amazing that I'd never broken a bone. Then I got a little too ambitious playing jump rope with Hutton one weekend and broke my foot. The cast was unwieldy and a real pain. I had to hobble around with great difficulty for a few weeks. Ten days or so after the accident, Stu and I were taking the two little ones out to TGI Friday's for dinner. Because of my injury, Stu dropped the kids and me at the entrance to the restaurant and drove off to park the car.

It was a busy Friday night, and the waiting area was crowded with couples and families waiting for a table. I approached the hostess and put our name in for a party of four. Literally, in the ninety seconds that my back was turned, the two kids started fighting. It started with a shove, and soon turned into a huge brawl. I turned around to see C.J. and Hutton punching each other as hard as they could in the middle of the crowded room. I could not believe my eyes.

I walked back to them as fast as I could and grabbed one kid in each hand. I pulled them apart, whipped them around, and hobbled outside, holding them in a death grip. Sure enough, along came Stu, walking toward the restaurant whistling, ready for a nice meal. He stopped in confusion when he saw me standing there with a very unpleasant look on my face.

"Please go back and get the car. We're going home," I told him.

"What's the matter? What happened in there?" he asked.

"Let them tell you . . . but we are leaving. Can you please go get the car?"

God bless Stu, he didn't argue. He turned right back around and retrieved the car. Meanwhile, I stood at the entrance to the restaurant with C.J. and Hutton, who had most definitely quieted down. In fact, they were petrified. They were in big trouble, and they knew it. Stu pulled up, we all got into the car, and Stu pulled out of the lot.

"Okay, what happened in there?" he asked. I told him about the scene in the restaurant. "We are going straight home. I will not go out with them if that's the way they behave in a restaurant. That behavior is absolutely not tolerable." I was furious with both of them.

Stu agreed completely. We drove home with the two kids crying in the backseat the whole way. They were out of luck. We returned to the apartment where they each got a sandwich and were sent straight to bed. Hutton and C.J. were certainly cowed; they apologized over and over. So much for a nice family night out. As Stu and I sat at the kitchen table wondering what we were going to eat, I had to laugh. "You know what I've just realized, Stu? I really love those kids. I know I do because I want to kill them right now!"

It was a stunning realization. I didn't just enjoy their company or tolerate them as part of the package. I loved these kids—unconditionally, the way I loved my own kids. To their credit, they respected what I said. Even that night, there was never any attitude along the lines of, "You're not my mother!" or "I don't have to listen to you!" Stu and I put up a united front. Not once did they go to him and try to get around anything I said.

I was always very straightforward. "I'm not your mother. You have a mother who loves you, and I'm not trying to replace her. You know I love your dad, and I want to spend time with you, but there are rules here. I'm not picking on you. Ask Paul and Jessica about the rules if you don't believe me!" The kids sensed the love I had for their father and appreciated it. I had thought I was done raising children, but life was full of surprises.

CHAPTER 12

STU TO THE RESCUE

Nine months after I met him, Stu and I were very happily living together in his apartment, and my bond with his children continued to grow. Jessica was doing very well at college in Santa Barbara. I remained concerned about Paul, who lived and worked with his father, but he was all grown-up, so there was nothing much I could do. Stu and I grew closer and closer. My biggest fear—all the baggage I brought with me because of Joey—began to seem unfounded as life unwound peacefully.

It was so peaceful, in fact, that it was difficult for me to adjust to such a calm relationship. Stu didn't tell me that he loved me ten times a day. He didn't make over-the-top declarations about how beautiful I was all the time, or remind me constantly that he could not live without me. He didn't come home with extravagant gifts for no reason. I had only known one kind of relationship—the roller-coaster. It was hard for me to fathom that love could be this comfortable and relaxed. After nearly a year of cohabitation, it was time to take the next step: a trip together to Long Island, where we'd both grown up. Stu was aware that my parents were very religious Catholics as he had heard quite a bit about them from the kids and me. My parents knew all about Stu, of course, and understood that our relationship was very serious. My mother, still smarting over the fact that I was divorced, couldn't help making some remarks along the lines of, "Well, you could get an annulment, and Stu could convert to Catholicism . . ." but I cut them right off.

"Mom—I don't care. Why should anyone we want to marry have to convert to our religion? What's wrong with being Jewish or Buddhist or anything else for that matter? Stu is an amazing person, a great father, and so different from Joe! No one's annulling anything or converting to or from anything!" I stood up to her on this one, but, laughable as it sounds, I couldn't work up the courage to tell them we lived together. Divorcing had been bad enough. I couldn't bear to hear what they'd say about this living arrangement.

Stu could not believe that at the age of nearly fifty I wouldn't tell my own parents that we were living in sin. They always called my cell phone, so I was spared having to explain the move to them. It was much easier just to maintain the fiction that I still had my own place in Newport Beach. Stu found the situation ridiculous. "You've got to tell them we live together, here in my place!"

"No way, Stu. Not because I'm scared . . . but because I don't want to hear it."

We started the official "Meet Stu" tour on Long Island, where Stu met my sisters in addition to Joe's sister Anne and her husband. Joe had given everybody such a run for their money, and it was obvious how happy we were together, so everybody welcomed Stu warmly. We took a little driving tour, with me pointing out my old school, church, and the infamous house. I had avoided this neighborhood like the plague for six long years—seeing it would have been just too sad. I had been so happy here; I could not have imagined another life. But I'd never had anything to compare it to. I was now with a new man, a new family, living an entirely different life thousands of miles away. I was content. Seeing all the old landmarks, which looked exactly the same, brought only a slight feeling of melancholy. This life didn't fit me anymore.

"Hey, let's stop by the auto body shop," Stu suggested. "We're right here in town."

"I have no desire to go there," I said. "I *can't* go in there."

"Mary Jo. You've got to go see Bobby. Come on."

"I don't want to, Stu. I'm ashamed. Joey messed up everything so badly and nearly destroyed everything that Dad ever built."

"You have nothing to be ashamed of. The two of you not talking is crazy. We're here; we're going to see Bobby." He drove to Complete Auto Body and parked. "Get out of this car and go talk to your brother," he insisted. So I did.

Bobby and I had not spoken in nearly eight years. His wife Ursula happened to be standing behind the counter when I walked through the door, and her face lit up when she saw me. We embraced, and the initial awkwardness quickly disappeared. Bobby was out on a call, but he soon returned, and the three of us had a good, long talk. "I'm so sorry, Bobby. I was just so ashamed," I told him.

He couldn't understand that. "Why were *you* ashamed?" he asked.

"Because I stayed," I said. "Because I kept thinking I could change him, that things would get better."

Bobby, Ursula, and I really hashed everything out, and all of us learned several things about what had really happened during my marriage. They had no idea that our first house had been sold to Joe's coke dealer. "He told us he planned to open his own business!" Bobby said. "He told Dad that if he didn't get the money to start his own business on the spot, he'd sell his shares in Complete Auto Body back to the original owner. We never heard anything about selling the house to a dealer!" Both of them were shocked by this story.

When I made a passing reference to the fact that I completely understood why Ursula had been forced to put her foot down and refuse to let Joe work at the shop after his jail term, Bobby looked at me incredulously. "Ursula had nothing to do with it; it was all me! It was my business, my decision. She didn't say anything about it! After he got arrested in L.A., I was done; I couldn't deal with him anymore. People were driving by, throwing eggs, coming in and pointing and making fun of us . . . I needed to make a living! I went to see him in jail and told him he couldn't come back!"

How well I remembered all of Joe's bitter complaints about Ursula and the fact that an outsider was taking away his birthright. They'd been endless and had eventually worked me into a righteous state of anger, too. Bobby and I had both been so wrapped up in our separate miseries that it had been easy to drive a wedge between us. That had been Joe's genius. One story to his brother and father, another to his wife, and both had been convincing enough to make us feel awkward and uncomfortable around each other—so much so that we'd become estranged, which was Joe's whole intent. This way, no one would ever compare stories. Bobby and I were both taken aback by each other's revelations.

The meeting ended warmly, with promises to remain in touch. An old, nagging hurt had been healed, and I had Stu to thank for the return of a long-lost family member.

～᠗

Next it was time to drive to rural Maine. Stu was a wreck, picturing Christians holding up crosses at the door when he entered or something. His imagination was running wild. I kept trying to reassure him that it would all turn out fine, and that my parents, while religious, were lovely people. He wasn't sure; he had heard some stories.

The first thing my father said to Stu when they met was, "Let's get one thing straight. Call me Dad." It set the tone for a delightful visit. As I observed them together over the next few days, it occurred to me that Stu was in many ways like my father: honest, hardworking, and an upstanding citizen. Not the most exotic traits, but after you live with a sociopath, these were all new to me. Stu and I didn't have huge ups and downs, a fact I was just beginning to adjust to. Because I had never known what it was like to have a reliable partner, for months I had unconsciously braced myself, waiting for the shoe to drop. Seeing him with my parents gave me a hopeful glimpse of the future: Stu would always be right there, steady and reliable, just as my father had been at my mother's side for nearly fifty years.

"Mom, I'm going to tell you this now," I said one day, as we sat in the kitchen. "Stu and I live together."

"I know, Mary Jo. What did you think, I didn't know that?" she laughed. This was a very encouraging reaction, but I wanted to really get things straight once and for all. No more ignoring inconvenient facts or pretending they weren't there or hadn't happened. I wanted to hammer the point home that I was capable of making my own decisions and fully intended to do so, and I wasn't going to be afraid to tell my own mother about them, either. I would no longer permit myself to live in fear of her reactions.

"Mom, Stu's been very concerned that I haven't told you this before. But I didn't tell you because I didn't want to be read the riot act. I love you, but I am now a middle-aged woman with grown children and gray hair. Believe what you want to believe, and live exactly how you want to—and I'm going to do the same. I know you don't approve of divorce or living in sin, but living with Stu is the right choice for me. Anything you say won't change that. I love him, and I want to be with him, and that's how it is."

It was a strong speech, one I would have been completely incapable of making even a year or so before, when I'd dared to speak up to my mother for the first time. I refused to live in fear of what my parents thought or said any longer. I had completely broken free of the need for Mommy and Daddy's approval—the pattern I constantly returned to— and, like that, my comfort zone was gone. I appreciated that my mother has a very strong faith, which is a tremendous source of comfort and strength to her. But my path wasn't hers, and for the second time in my life—it only took fifty years—I made it clear to her that I was going to live for myself and make my own decisions about what was best for me from that point on. I was officially a grown-up.

Our visit back East was a stunning success in every way.

The quiet life was nice while it lasted—until December 2003. That's when everything fell to pieces, as it inevitably had to. I was out shopping for Christmas presents one morning, listening to a CD of carols in the car as I drove to the mall, when Stu called. "Do you have the radio on?" he asked. I didn't like the tone of his voice. Something was up.

"No," I said hesitantly. "What's the matter?"

"Joey just got busted for insurance fraud by the FBI, and they raided his house. It's all over the news."

I felt sick to my stomach, a familiar feeling. Paul lived there, and I was sure he was on the scene. I knew Jessica was spending her winter break from school at her father's house, and I prayed that she wasn't there. It was very likely that she was at a friend's house instead. I dialed her cell phone several times, but she didn't answer. I grew more and more agitated, picturing her sleeping late as I tried to reach her and break the news. I tried Paul's number, too, and only got his voice mail.

I headed for Stu's office, where the staff was hard at work. I ran inside, absolutely frantic because I couldn't reach either of my kids. My cell phone was ringing constantly with friends trying to alert me. Helicopters were buzzing overhead, and reporters were all over the scene, both at Joe's home and the nearby body shop. I wanted nothing more than to race to the house and see for myself what was going on, but Stu convinced me to stay away. "The media will be all over you, and they won't let you in anyway." He was right, but I felt frantic and helpless as we sat and waited and watched the television coverage.

At the end of the very long day, Jessica and Paul's girlfriend at the time, Jamie, burst in, still wearing their pajamas. They'd been sitting around the whole day in the clothes they were wearing at 6:00 AM, when they'd been literally pulled out of bed by FBI agents. Both were crying and near hysterical. Jessie had been forced to sit on a couch in her father's living room for five hours in her pajamas while I had no idea where she was.

"They wouldn't let me answer my phone, Mom! I kept telling them, 'That's my mother calling, and she's worried because she doesn't know where I am!' They didn't care!"

We put the girls in an empty office and did our best to comfort them and calm them down. Their presence was disruptive to the office, to say the least. My relief was overwhelming, but then panic set in. This was my boyfriend's place of business. I had brought utter chaos to the place, and no one had gotten any work done all day. How could they? Stu was most certainly getting the true picture of what life with Joey was like.

Paul, too, was eventually released and showed up at Stu's office. He looked pale and drained, which was to be expected, as he'd been woken out of a sound sleep by men standing over his bed, pointing guns at him and shouting, "FBI! Freeze!" He, too, had been virtually held hostage all day, until Joe was eventually taken away. As I fussed anxiously around him, he said wearily, "It's all right, Mom. In fact, I'm glad this happened. It's finally over." Then he headed downtown to jail to bail out his old man.

As an employee of Joey's auto body shop in the Valley, Paul had gotten a good up-close look at what was going on, and he hated it. Padded bills, insurance fraud, shady dealings . . . he protested loudly and often. But when you're twenty-one years old and your father, who also happens to be your boss, is telling you that you should stop worrying so much, it's hard to keep fighting. The arguments always ended the same way, with Joe telling him, "This is my shop, and we do things my way. When you have to pay all the bills, then you can do things your way. Until that day, you do what I say."

But after a really bad fight, Joe would show up the next day and put his arms around Paul. "It's been rough around here lately. You need a break. Take some time off and go to Hawaii for a week," and hand over two first-class tickets to Maui. Or present the keys to a new car. It's hard to turn down that kind of inducement when you're twenty-one years old. The constant stress and tension of waiting for the house of cards to collapse had made Paul very sick. No wonder the FBI raid came as somewhat of a relief.

My nerves were absolutely shot, not least because one of my worst fears had been realized: How would the new man in my life react to this insanity? Who would put up with this kind of chaos? How embarrassing and mortifying that this was my ex-husband! Thank God Stu was in it for the long haul. He was more upset by how upset the kids and I were than any inconvenience we caused his company. I wasn't living with Joe anymore. We were officially divorced, but his life would never fail to affect mine.

It didn't end that day. For months, the legal wrangling went back and forth. Court dates, lawyers, pleadings, you name it. It was very familiar and tiring. Joey called me frequently to complain. The authorities were plotting against him, as always. It wasn't his fault, of course. He hadn't done anything wrong. The usual. He was eventually sentenced to one year in prison.

Stu and I were gravely concerned about Paul, who rapidly spiraled downward into a very dark place. His whole life collapsed the day of the FBI raid. Given his father's troubles, he soon had no job and no place to live. Once again, Paul started drinking heavily and obliterating his mind with drugs. It was a repeat of his first dreadful year in a California high school, only this time the stakes were much higher. He was in the middle of a complete breakdown. It was plain to see that he was in a great deal of pain, and I visited him frequently at his temporary place—his girlfriend's apartment. She was just as much at a loss as I was in terms of how to help him. Neither of us could get through.

He spent the time he wasn't out getting drugs lying in a darkened bedroom. He made no attempt to get a job but lived off the money he'd saved. Eventually, of course, it ran out, and soon enough the fancy truck his father had bought him was repossessed. Stu was anxious to step in and at least stave that off, but I refused to let him. I had learned a thing or two about enabling in my life. We agonized about Paul's situation, but allowed the consequences to unfold.

Painful as it was to see my son like this, as badly as I wanted to fix everything and make it all better, I knew I couldn't. "You're a man now, Paul, and you've got two good arms and legs and a brain. I know all too well what you're going through, but there will come a time when you can't use this as an excuse anymore. Your father screwed up your childhood and young adulthood, no doubt about it. Don't let him be the reason the rest of your life is a disaster, too. The choice is in your hands," I told him over and over.

Practicing tough love on my son was one of the hardest things I had ever done. Stu wanted to give him money, move him into the house we'd bought together, anything and everything. But I stuck to my guns, even though for months I was worried sick. If I'd had any doubts before about my future with Stu, they disappeared forever at this time. During this crisis, Stu once again demonstrated the true measure of his character.

Just like his mother, Paul eventually, begrudgingly, decided to get back up and start living again. Stu gave Paul work at his printing office and taught him how to work many different computer programs. He listened to Paul and did his best to offer support and advice. He was there for my son all the time, serving as a guide and role model, something his father had failed miserably to do. It was all Paul had ever wanted. I didn't think I could love Stu more, but this sealed the deal.

It was a terrible year for my son, with plenty of fits and starts, but by early 2005, Paul, through sheer willpower, pulled himself up by his bootstraps and began to turn his life around step-by-step. He had some help from Stu and me, of course—we were only too happy to do all we could for him once we saw him making an effort to help himself. He found an office job at a major corporation—as far away from the auto repair industry as he could get—and began to lay the groundwork for a new career. He moved into an apartment with some roommates, and though they were all young and liked to go out and have fun, he was on the right track. I could not have been more proud of him. He had been badly scarred by the years of living and working with his father, where there was little structure, stability, and appropriate father/son boundaries.

I had just begun to relax and allow myself to stop worrying about my son when I was hit with sad news about my father. The shock I felt on hearing he'd been diagnosed with terminal cancer was aggravated by the difficulty I had traveling back and forth to Maine. For the hundredth time, I wished I lived nearby so that I could spend more quality time with him when it became clear he was nearing the end of his life. I also felt deeply for my mother and would have liked to do more for her. I took some comfort in the fact that my father and I had had such a revealing conversation a couple of years before—the closest one we'd ever had—and that he and Stu had met and gotten on famously. I felt peaceful in the sense that there was nothing left unsaid between us.

Soon the end was very near, and I made plans to head to Maine for what would surely be my father's funeral. I have to say that Joe was very supportive when I called to inform him of the latest news, perhaps remembering when his own father had died of cancer. Joe made a point of always asking about him, checking on his health, and staying informed about the man who had been his father-in-law for nearly twenty-five years, which I appreciated. Of course, there was some unspoken resentment on my part, the feeling of *You're the reason I'm three thousand miles away while my father is dying! I can't sit around day after day and hold his hand like I did for yours!* These words lay unsaid between us, making him only too anxious to help. "Let me buy your plane ticket," Joe said. "No, no, I insist," he added, as I started to demur. "Now, listen, I'll be in San Diego this weekend, but here's a cell phone number. Call me to let me know you've arrived safely," he said before I left.

Of course, it's not easy to get to the boonies in Maine, so I planned to fly into New York on the red-eye, meet one of my sisters in the city, and drive with her to my parents' home, a nine-hour car trip but still the most efficient way to get us both there as soon as possible. Unfortunately, Dad had the audacity to die on Evanka's birthday, the day before I left. I got the call as I was packing. "Hold on, Mom, I'm on the way," I told her, wishing I was already there. I could only imagine her grief; she'd just lost her husband of fifty years.

I called Stu at his office, my children, and Joe, just to be polite. He answered the phone, I broke the news, and he said, "Oh, Mary Jo, I'm so sorry." I heard a lot of squawking in the background, and he shouted, "I *know* it's your birthday . . . her father just died!" Then back to me, "Go ahead, tell me what your plans are now."

"Ummm, am I interrupting something?" I asked.

"No, no, it's fine, don't worry about it . . . he was a good man . . ." We had a couple of minutes of social niceties and then I hung up. Evanka was screaming at him at the top of her lungs in the background the whole time we were on the phone—all three minutes. Joe had met his match in this one—they had a fiery relationship, to say the least. She gave as good as she got. I had never met her, but I heard plenty from those who did, particularly my children. I was very far from being the scorned or jealous ex-wife. I actually would have liked it if Paul and Jessica could've gotten along with their father's new wife. But it was clear that was never going to happen. In fact, it was still unclear as to the relationship my children would have with their own father, now that they were adults themselves.

The consensus among experts in the field, including Dr. Martha Stout in her brilliant book, *The Sociopath Next Door*, is that those stuck in a relationship with a sociopath should run, not walk, away from them—for good. Not that it's easy, but adults can manage to do this through separation and divorce. The problem becomes compounded when children are involved. Paul and Jessica had been traumatized as children by the Amy Fisher matter, and then further scarred by ongoing life with Joey. Still, he was their father, and he constantly assured them both how much he loved them. All I could say as they became adults was what I truly believed: Joe's actions spoke much louder than the endless explanations and justifications coming out of his mouth. If our son and daughter wanted to maintain some kind of relationship with their father, I was all for it, but they should remember: as long as they didn't believe a word he said, they would never be disappointed again.

CHAPTER 13

THE LIFE LIFT

Several weeks after my father's funeral, I turned fifty, complete with a huge family party thrown by my new family. That September, word got out that Amy Fisher would soon be appearing on *Oprah* to promote her new book. The news absolutely stunned me. This wasn't Jerry Springer; this was Oprah, queen of the book clubs, thoughtful influencer of millions of women and readers worldwide. Many family members and friends of mine were outraged and e-mailed Oprah's producers to express their dismay. Of all the people in the world Oprah might choose to highlight, of all the thousands and thousands of worthy books out there, why was this one so appealing?

Jessica, at college in Santa Barbara, was particularly unhappy about this news. She fired off an angry e-mail saying, "I am outraged that Oprah, who I have always admired and looked up to as a woman of character, could stoop so low as to have an attempted murderer on her show to promote her book." One of Oprah's senior producers, Brian Piotrowicz, contacted Jessica and told her, "In the interest of fairness, we'd love to have your mother on the show too—and you, Jessica, are welcome to join her." Jessica became very excited.

"Mom, Mom, we could be on *Oprah*!" she said when she called me. "We don't have to be in the same room as Amy, of course . . . we'd be separate. It could be really great . . ."

"No, Jessica," I told her firmly. "I've been around the media for way too long, and I know how producers think and work. Of course they'd love to get the two of us together somehow! I am absolutely not going on the show, and I would advise you not to either. It's just not a winning situation for you no matter how you behave." I didn't want her put in the uncomfortable position of defending her father and braving a firestorm of criticism—one I knew all too well.

Jessica was disappointed, but understood, and told Brian no. However, he stayed in contact with her, and they remained occasional correspondents. The show featuring Amy Fisher and her new book went ahead as scheduled, and I can't say Oprah was particularly nice or welcoming to her. That much, at least, made me happy. Oprah certainly didn't seem to embrace her or champion her book. Jessica got a bright idea and shared it with Oprah's producer: "All these extreme makeover shows are so big right now, and it got me to thinking. My mother just turned fifty, and I would love to give her a complete head-to-toe makeover. Her self-confidence is low because of other people's actions. I miss the vibrant, confident woman she used to be. I want to give her a Life Lift!"

Amazingly enough, the *Oprah* producers responded, and Jessica called me, absolutely thrilled beyond words this time, and explained the whole concept to me. Of course, I'd have to appear on the show, probably more than once, and dig up many matters that I preferred not to go into. It had been a long, hard road to arrive at this place of peace and acceptance. Why stir it all back up?

I discussed the idea with Stu and my mother and sisters. Eventually, I decided to go ahead and do it—as long as it was on my own terms. This meant not appearing with Amy or Joe—this show was going to be about *me* and my point of view. The producers were anxious to have Jessica appear, too, as it would be a newsworthy first. Jessica, at age twenty-two, had never spoken publicly about her feelings before, and this was one of the biggest stages in the world. Paul didn't want anything to do with it. "Have a good time, ladies, but it's not my thing," he said.

The show was set to air in November, during the all-important sweeps week. Stu, Jessica, and I flew to Chicago where we were put up at a luxury hotel. I was pre-interviewed the night before by the personable Brian. Now, for those of you who have ever wondered or imagined, here's what it's like to be a guest on *The Oprah Winfrey Show*: The limousine arrived to pick us up at our hotel and drove through the busy Chicago streets to Harpo Studios. We entered through a back door, where we were checked for cameras and video recorders.

Security was understandably tight. We were ushered into one of the several green rooms to await our turn. I realized while sitting there that Oprah actually tapes two or three shows a day when she's working, making for very long days for her. Bestselling author Terry McMillan, author of *How Stella Got Her Groove Back*, was also appearing that day to discuss her ill-fated marriage to a much younger man who had turned out to be gay. I was thrilled and flattered when she came into our green room to find me. She wanted to meet me! She couldn't have been nicer.

I started to get butterflies as we were taken to get our hair and makeup done. *It's taped,* I kept reminding myself. Taped before a live audience, of course, but I knew that if I really screwed up, it wouldn't be going out live all over America. I held on to that fact as we got closer and closer to our call time.

There's no chitchat or running into Oprah before the show. We wouldn't see her until we were on the air. I was taken to my chair on Oprah's set with very little fanfare. I looked out at the audience; they looked back at me. Suddenly, Oprah appeared and took her seat. I was stunned at how beautiful she was in person. Given all the endless coverage of her weight, I was also surprised to see that she was not heavy. She was an absolutely regular-sized woman. Oprah launched right into a recap of the 1992 events, and we watched some old video that literally made me cringe. It had been taken in the summer following my shooting. My hair was buzzed off. I was much too thin, spoke with difficulty, and was corrosively angry. I was sure that the image of that woman was still what people saw when they heard my name, even though that was no longer me. In fact, I barely recognized that woman.

Then my chat with Oprah began—not my favorite topics, but she was most gracious. I was an old hand at being interviewed; it was my daughter I was worried about. What a place to have your first interview! The producers brought another chair over, and Jessica was brought out for the second segment. She came out looking beautiful and calm, but I could see her hands shaking. She was extremely nervous, of course, but did quite well. At one point, Oprah asked Jessica what she thought about the interview she had conducted with Amy and Jessica's opinion of Amy today. "There's no soul there. It's kind of like the mall's open, but nobody's shopping." The audience laughed.

"The mall's open, but nobody's shopping! Mmmm, mmmm, mmm! I like that, Jessica!" Oprah liked that line, and Jessica was immediately much more at ease. She handled the rest of the interview like a pro. Dr. Robin joined us and analyzed Jessica's remarks about her father, making it very clear that in her professional opinion, Joe had not been a good father, no matter how Jessica felt. My daughter and I had decided together beforehand to be very careful and diplomatic in what we said about both Amy and Joey. I could see Jessie tense up again at Dr. Robin's words, but neither of us argued or defended anyone's actions. The show closed with a discussion of my recent milestone birthday and Jessica's wish to somehow give me a head-to-toe makeover.

At the conclusion of the interview, Oprah introduced Stu, who was sitting in the audience, and motioned for him to come up onstage. She held out her arm for him, and he escorted her off the stage—a lovely gesture on her part. We all trooped backstage, got our pictures taken, and she couldn't have been warmer or nicer. Then she was off to tape another show.

Unbeknownst to me, a woman named Jessica Azizzadeh was sitting at home in L.A, eight months pregnant with her second child, watching *Oprah* that afternoon. Her husband, Dr. Babek Azizzadeh, happens to be one of the top plastic surgeons in California. He specialized in facial reconstruction of nerve damage and facial deformities. Dr. Azizzadeh did far more than beautify pampered women in Beverly Hills; he traveled extensively around the globe consulting on the most difficult cases in the most remote third-world countries, providing cleft palate and other surgeries for those who would otherwise have no hope. He was interested in the challenge my lopsided face presented, so he phoned the *Oprah* show and said, "I would like to help Mary Jo. I know I can do something for her."

~~

A few days after we arrived back home in Los Angeles, I was given the doctor's number by an *Oprah* producer and invited to visit his office in Beverly Hills for a consult. Now, I have known some real devils in my life, but Dr. Azizzadeh was a true angel sent from heaven. Dr. Azizzadeh only knew what he'd read about in the tabloids years before, so he was quite curious to meet me. I'm sure he wondered if I was totally sane and well enough for plastic surgery. He soon learned that I was. We hit it off immediately.

The more I learned about his practice, the more impressed I became. Dr. Azizzadeh is tremendously admired and respected in the medical community, and he put together a top-notch team of physicians to make me over from head to toe. "Mary Jo," he said to me, "tell me everything you want." What an invitation!

He assembled the most amazing team of surgeons, including an eye doctor, an ear specialist, and a throat doctor to collaborate with him on my case. Together they came up with a very ambitious plan to fix me up—both functionally and aesthetically. He determined that I was psychologically healthy and realistic about my looks. The damage to my face and the ongoing aging process were both facts of life I had reluctantly accepted long before, so I was an excellent candidate. I was awestruck that all these brilliant doctors wanted to do something for me. They wanted to fix me, help me, and make me look and feel better.

My days were jammed with endless doctors' appointments. I had plenty of experience with doctors and surgical procedures, of course, but this was something new. All of this surgery was cosmetic and elective, which many people tend to take lightly, but it was very serious. It can sound very casual when people discuss it—"Oh, I'm just getting a nip and tuck"—but all surgery has risks and possible complications. We see tragedies in the news all the time—Kanye West's mother being the latest high-profile example. A good plastic surgeon does everything in his power to ensure that his patients are viable candidates. If there are any medical problems or foreseeable complications, they will refuse to perform elective surgery. Dr. Azizzadeh was the best—the screening was extensive. I agreed that the entire process from start to finish could be taped for a future *Oprah* show. Suddenly, I was the star of my own little reality show. At every blood test, consultation, and doctor's meeting, a cameraman trailed behind me.

Jeremy Fine, M.D., was the ridiculously young and handsome internist who supervised my general overall health. He also happened to be single. I was so taken by him that I immediately wanted to hook him up with my daughter. I underwent extensive medical tests to be sure I could handle more surgery. I was going to undergo eight hours under anesthesia with three separate operations. He made sure there were absolutely no underlying problems. He ordered blood work, EKGs, and every conceivable kind of test, including a mammogram at the Beverly Tower Women's Center before approving breast surgery, which was exactly what every good plastic surgeon requires. Fortunately, I was as healthy as a horse.

Dr. Lance Wyatt was a wonderful plastic surgeon. His office staff was simply amazing, and he did the most beautiful body work. Menopause had hit me hard, and I had gotten quite soft.

I always worked out, but I had "things" on my sides that I could not get rid of no matter what I did. He promised me that liposuction would make them disappear. He also promised to give my breasts a lift.

It became very clear to me how revered Dr. Azizzadeh was as I met with all these other doctors. Each and every one of them was happy to do anything with him and for him because he had such a stellar reputation. William Slattery was a renowned ear specialist at the House Clinic Los Angeles. The ear problems I'd had since the shooting were the most debilitating to my daily life. My previous operations had left me with an ear canal that was so full of scar tissue that it had shrunk to nothing more than a tiny pinprick hole. Ear infections were just a part of my life. Every now and then, my ear would start oozing, and I'd have to rush to the doctor to have it cleaned out. My ear canal could no longer drain itself properly and was a constant source of pain and aggravation. The pain when my ear became infected was agonizing, but just something I had learned to accept. I was also completely deaf in that ear, but I had adjusted to that, as well.

Dr. Slattery conducted a number of hearing tests on me, and we discussed the possibility of a state-of-the-art cochlear implant to cure my deafness. When I learned what was involved—actually screwing the implant into the skull and snapping a tiny hearing implement on and off—I decided it wasn't for me. I had more or less adjusted to complete hearing loss in one ear. The thought of screwing anything into my skull made me nervous. I appreciated that these implants were an amazing invention, but I had learned to compensate for the hearing loss. Dr. Slattery could easily see that the pinhole opening was causing all the other problems, so he planned to open up the hole in my ear canal, thus making it possible for me to clean it with a Q-tip.

The right side of my throat was completely paralyzed, and even now I had a great deal of trouble swallowing. I had learned to compensate over the years by taking smaller bites, chewing longer, and always drinking water with meals because food goes down very slowly when I swallow. One half of my throat was doing all the work instead of both sides. Dr. David Alessi did a barium swallow test to follow exactly what was going on and, among other tips, taught me to turn my head as I swallowed. It was just a simple trick, but it made food go down so much more easily. Dr. Theresa England from Premier Surgery worked with me on physical therapy exercises to loosen my facial paralysis and allow the muscles to move more freely. They had many innovative ideas on how to stretch, move, and work those damaged muscles.

Dr. Robert Sachs performed Lasik surgery on my eyes. The nerves in my right eye had been damaged, of course, and much of that could not be repaired. He did a number of tests on my vision to adjust the Lasik for my injury, which made it quite a bit more complicated than usual. Nicholas Manley, Dr. Azizzadeh's right-hand man, was my rock throughout. I absolutely adored him. He kept all my appointments straight through the Lapeer Surgical Center, where my surgery took place with this team of premier doctors. When the big day arrived, a camera crew from *Oprah* taped my entire eight-hour surgery, which is quite a long time to be knocked out and under the knife. There was extensive work to be done, and every minute was painstakingly scheduled to allow each doctor to work in his or her particular area of specialty.

MARY JO'S LIFE LIFT:

Pre-testing, blood work, overall health supervision (Dr. Jeremy Fine)

Liposuction and breast lift (Dr. Lance Wyatt)

Neck lift, facelift, upper and lower eyelid surgery, chemical peel, Botox injections (Dr. Babak Azizzedeh)

Reconstruction of right ear canal (Dr. William Slattery)

Facial muscle stimulation, throat barium test (Dr. David Alessi, Dr. Theresa England)

Lasik eye surgery (Dr. Robert Sachs)

Hairstyling (Yuki Sharoni Beauty and Lifestyle Salon and Spa—Beverly Hills)

Stu, naturally, was very worried. It was a major eight-hour surgery, and he was afraid of the effects of the anesthesia—that I wouldn't wake up or that something would go wrong. I didn't want him sitting outside waiting for eight long hours. There was nothing he could do. I insisted he go to work just like he would on a regular day. I later learned that the staff checked in by phone with him every hour, giving him updates. "She's doing great; they're working on her ear right now." An hour later, "All is well. Dr. Wyatt is doing her liposuction for the next half hour." They continually assured him that I was in the best hands, just one more example of their outstanding consideration.

I can't say I felt too hot when I woke up, and I looked like I'd emerged from a very bad car accident. The one good thing about my history was the fact that I'd been seriously hurt before. I had known going into this exactly what I was signing on for. This, too, would pass, and the amazing power of the human body to recover would soon kick in. Still, all those procedures really kicked my ass. Fortunately, I was whisked off to a medical recovery facility for three days where I was cared for by the kindest nurses I have ever known. I was thankful for the extra-special coddling—not to mention that this recovery period spared Stu and my kids the sight of me immediately following major surgery. I was quite a sight.

Serenity Surgery Aftercare Facility was a wonderful haven. I could not have possibly dreamed of being so pampered. When I arrived, I was wrapped up like a mummy, and it was an ordeal just to go to the bathroom. The nurses were with me every minute. Had I not been so beaten up from the surgery, my stay would have been just like visiting a top-notch spa. Ladies, if you're getting extensive surgery, I cannot recommend this aftercare enough. I didn't want to leave! But leave I did, to continue recovering at home. I anxiously waited to see if a butterfly would emerge from this cocoon!

I had been a bit self-conscious about my facial injury for years—and no one likes getting old and saggy—but I had so much to be grateful for. I could walk, I could talk, my brain still worked, and I had a mate who loved me exactly as I was, so why complain? Many people endured terrible tragedies in their lives. I didn't have it any worse—I actually had it much better—than plenty of people out there. Yes, I lost part of my hearing for good. Yes, half of my face was frozen permanently, but I had adjusted to those realities because I had no choice. I had to.

I was officially divorced and in a loving, healthy relationship. My children had weathered the storm and were doing well. I had made peace with my parents and Amy Fisher. I no longer wallowed in the past. I didn't mope around pitying myself anymore. I believe that this change in attitude is why I was given the most wonderful gift of what I called my Life Lift. Out of the blue, the most brilliant and dedicated doctors appeared and wanted to help me. From the nurses, to the operating room staff, to the recovery room, every last person I met was so kind, loving, and anxious to do something good for *me*. I was completely taken aback by their skill and generosity. It was almost too much to be the recipient of all this largesse. I knew I would never be able to adequately express my appreciation.

As the months passed and I healed completely, I was even more awed by the talent of all my doctors. I looked amazing! I also felt better than I had since the day, I was shot. From the moment I awoke, I noticed a major difference in my ear. To this day, I suffer from minor ear infections that cause some pain, but the contrast is night and day. Now I can address the problem myself with a Q-tip and drops. The discomfort is fleeting, and there have been no more horrendous infections. That particular surgery changed my life in a very profound way. Dr. Slattery addressed the lingering trauma of the bullet injury. And Dr. Sachs made it possible for me to read again without glasses, a wonderful benefit for me! Finally, the Botox Dr. Azizzadeh injected worked on my nerves in the exact opposite way it works on most people—instead of freezing the muscle, it relaxed the damaged nerves and provided me relief I hadn't felt in years. I had never even dreamed of such a transformation.

Restoring my looks, and the functionality of my facial muscles and hearing, restored an inner confidence that I hadn't felt since before the shooting. I had done so much emotional work on myself in the years I'd been separated from Joey. This Life Lift was the cherry on top of the cake, and I believe was only bestowed on me because I was emotionally ready: the outside now matched the inside. I literally glowed from within. I was certainly appreciative. When you've been really down and out, like I had felt many times in my life, you don't take the good times for granted. They are a magical gift to be savored. I was amazed and humbled by the beauty in my life.

I was scheduled to return to do a follow-up on *Oprah* during sweeps week in May 2006, six months after my surgery. A couple of months before my appearance, I got a call from a producer at *Entertainment Tonight* (*ET*). He was proposing that Amy Fisher, Joe, and I all get together in one room and face each other in person for the first time since 1992. He was sure that the ratings for this reunion on the fourteenth anniversary of the shooting would be out of sight. I had absolutely no interest in the idea. Furthermore, I was legally prohibited from appearing on any television show until after my second appearance on *Oprah*. It was part of my contract. *Oprah* had made all the arrangements to give me this Life Lift and, reasonably enough, didn't want anyone getting a peek at the "new" me until after I was unveiled on her show. I told them absolutely no way, hung up, and forgot about it.

But *ET* wouldn't give up. Producers began calling me daily, begging me to take part in this show. At some point I learned that Joey and Amy had both signed on and agreed to sit down and face each other. As usual when it came to publicity, I was the wet blanket. I explained over and over that I had no desire to see Amy Fisher in person ever again in my life and had zero desire to appear with the two of them on this or any other show. "Even if I wanted to do it, I can't! I am legally and contractually bound to *Oprah* until my follow-up episode airs in May! How many times do I have to explain this?!"

Even without my participation, the hype for the show was huge. Teasers were aired on *ET* weeks in advance, and the producers stretched out the Joey/Amy confrontation over two long weeks in May. I watched several of the shows before I left for Chicago and just shook my head. The two of them fought and hurled insults at each other. It was embarrassing. Meanwhile, the calls kept coming. *ET* still hoped I would agree to an appearance. I flew to Chicago on a Wednesday and taped at Oprah's studio on a Thursday.

This was the big "after" show, where they played footage of my doctors' meetings and surgery and talked to Dr. Azizzadeh about what exactly he'd done and why. I made my grand entrance at the end to show off my new look. My hair was styled, I wore a new outfit, and I was literally queen for the day. I looked great, and Dr. Azizzadeh was thrilled with the results. The man is a genius. I didn't look pulled too tight or overdone in any way. I simply looked younger, rejuvenated, and similar to the pretty young woman I'd been before I was shot. The peace, calmness, and contentment in my life were now accurately reflected on my face.

When I got back to my hotel after the taping, I had literally a dozen messages from *ET* producers saying they would work around my schedule if I would just meet with Joey and Amy for a couple of hours. I was feeling very strong, happy about my new look, and ready and able to face anything. Maybe, I mused, it wasn't such a bad idea. Maybe I could get an answer or two to some of the questions I still had. At the very least, I could lend a bit of dignity to the proceedings, so that Paul and Jessica could see one of their parents behaving properly. When they called me back yet again, I agreed to make one appearance, for one hour only. I would listen to what Amy had to say, listen to what Joe had to say, and then leave. That was it.

Needless to say, the show's producers were ecstatic.

I flew home to Los Angeles that night and had barely tumbled into bed when a limousine picked me up at 5:00 AM on Friday, the day my *Oprah* show aired across the nation. Stu and I were driven to a mansion in the Hollywood Hills, where *ET* was taping the show. I was immediately hustled off to my own room in the mansion. The producers were anxious to keep the three of us separated to preserve the tension—it would make great TV to capture my reunion with Amy. I was as cool as a cucumber. I was just going to listen, say my piece, and then go home and rest. They didn't want me to see Joey before the cameras rolled, either, but he threw a fit and swore he wouldn't go on until he spoke to me first. I rolled my eyes, and then went to see him.

Joey started talking nonstop the minute I saw him. He told me that he'd been very ill with diverticulosis. He'd been in the hospital, in fact, but had checked himself out just so he could be there for me. He was going on and on, and I just wanted to get on with the task at hand. I broke in and said, "I'm sorry to hear you're not feeling well." I no longer cared what he said about anything. I turned to one of the hovering producers. "Are we ready to go?"

I was brought to a huge empty room and placed on my mark. When Amy walked in, I walked right over to her. Very conscious that millions of people would see this on national television, I put out my arms and gave her a short hug. The truth is, as long and hard as I had worked at forgiving her, a big part of me still would have preferred to strangle her. But I knew I had to stay calm and collected. I absolutely refused to sink to their level.

Not surprisingly, Amy had no answers for me. She didn't know why she had done it. When I asked about the two boys she had tried to hire early on to shoot me, she refused to talk about them. When I asked about her father, she told me she hadn't come to talk about him. She was there to see me and tell me she was sorry in person. That was all. Amy was hard, cold, and evasive throughout the meeting. Ten minutes after laying eyes on her, I realized that the vague hope I might get any answers was foolish. This was a complete waste of my time. There was certainly no grand awakening on her part or mine.

Then Joe was brought in. He didn't last fifteen seconds before he stood up, grabbed his microphone, and threw it across the room, screaming, "Fuck you, you fucking cunt!" at Amy. He went off. I just sat in my chair next to his and looked straight ahead. The interview was over. I had no chance to see them interact in person together. Looking back, I should have known he'd do something to prevent me from asking them both questions they couldn't squirm or lie their way out of when all three of us were present. That was one thing Joey would prevent no matter what.

All the media excitement was over, and I returned with relief to my everyday life with Stu, looking and feeling fantastic. Joey's antics were the only fly in the ointment. It had been quite upsetting to Paul and Jessica, of course, when Joe had to serve his time for insurance fraud, but everyone had gotten through it. He hadn't even been out of prison for a year when I was sitting home one afternoon, minding my own business as usual, and got a call from one of my friends.

"Did you hear? Joey got arrested again," he said.

"What?" This was the *fourth time*. "What for?" Apparently, he had been busted on a parole violation. Joe had once again been put on probation for five years after serving the five-month sentence. Parole officers searching his house had uncovered a box of shotgun shells that went with an old rifle he'd once owned and promptly rearrested him. There were no actual guns there. It was ridiculous, not a big matter, but the damage was done.

I hung up the phone and called Stu into the room. "Stu, you are never going to believe this one!" I said, and related the story to him.

Stu just looked at me. "I can't believe this. What is wrong with him?"

Jessica happened to be at our house that day, sitting in the den doing her laundry and watching television. She was absorbed in some show when I walked into the room.

"Jess," I said, "I don't even know how to say this, so I'm just going to tell you straight out. Daddy got arrested again."

Jessica turned her head away from the screen and looked at me for a moment. "Who cares?" she said. "I've got laundry to do," and turned back to her program. I stood there for a moment and then went back to the living room to track down

Paul. When I got him on the phone and told him the news, he laughed. *Laughed.* "What the hell did he do now?"

Stu watched this with disbelief. "Mary Jo," he said after I'd hung up, "I don't think you realize how crazy this all is. If my mother called me and said my brother had been arrested, I would be going crazy. I'd be running around trying to get money, find him, you name it. One kid goes on with her laundry, the other just laughs, like this is a normal, everyday occurrence. No one's excited here. What is this, another day in the park?"

"Yes, Stu, this *is* normal—for Joey!"

All Stu could do was shake his head. The chaos was back on. Joe was soon calling me constantly to complain. He had to go back to jail, he'd lost his business, and he was on the verge of losing his huge house. I always tried to listen patiently and offer good advice, but every time I made a suggestion, he replied, "See, this is why we're not married anymore! I don't want to hear this!"

"Joe, then why do you call me and ask my opinion?" He really just wanted a shoulder to cry on while he went on about how everyone was out to get him. I wanted our relationship to remain amicable. I had tried to stay friendly with him for the sake of our children if nothing else, but his calls escalated in frequency and aggravation to the point that I realized I just couldn't do it anymore. I didn't want to hear his troubles about money, Evanka, the system that was out to get him— any of it! Talking to Joe was very upsetting to me, which upset Stu. My ex-husband continued to affect my life in a negative way. When push came to shove and Joe realized he had to sell his house, I got yet another jolt of bad news. It had been mortgaged to the hilt. There was literally not a penny to be made from its sale. I was due a certain percentage of the proceeds—it was all clearly spelled out in our divorce decree—but there was nothing to get. Enough was enough.

Same old broken record—me hysterical and disbelieving, Joe swearing up and down it wasn't his fault, the bank had screwed him, he hadn't done anything wrong . . . it was very stressful. My nerves were shot, I was drinking too much wine, and my relationship with Stu was suffering. We never argued or fought, but I was so drained from listening to Joey, worrying about the house sale, and fretting about the missing money that I had very little to offer Stu. When he wanted to go out to a movie or golfing for the day, I was always too tired. My mind was constantly racing; I was distracted and distant.

Then one day, the light came on. *Why am I in such a state because Joe's life is once again out of control? We're officially divorced—we don't live together anymore!* And just like that, I decided to stop taking his calls or interacting with him in any way. I'd spent so many years accepting all this chaos as normal that I habitually and unconsciously fell back into the groove. I had forgotten that I no longer had to be a part of it. I was free! I had been free for a long time, and from this point forward I was going to take advantage of it!

The next time Joe called, I didn't pick up the phone. When I listened to the message, it was very pleasant. "Hi, Mary Jo.

Just wanted to talk to you. Hope all is well. Call me back. Love you." He closed every conversation with these words, even now. I didn't return his call.

A few days later, he called again. "Uh, are we not speaking? Did we have a fight? Because you didn't return my call," he asked plaintively. "Give me a call. I need to speak with you." I didn't return that call either. Several more days passed. One more message.

"All right, well, if this is what you want to do, I won't bother you anymore. I'll leave you alone. You know where to find me if you need me. Love you." Click. And that was the end of that.

A lovely letter from him showed up a week or so later in the mail, containing a photo of me in kindergarten he'd held on to.

You were the most cutest kid in the class. You still are . . . Just thought you should have this.
All my love,
Joe

It was a beautiful letter, meant to tug at my heartstrings, and it did. I felt guilty for not calling him back. Cutting him off made me sad. But I just knew I couldn't do it anymore. The final layer of the onion had been peeled.

Joe returned to jail briefly for his parole violation. I was finally done. I washed my hands of the whole matter. But my former husband still had some surprises up his sleeve.

I felt I had had quite enough attention from the press given the huge ratings that the historic Joey/Amy/Mary Jo triangle, together again after fourteen years, had generated on *ET,* as well as my *Oprah* makeover. David Krieff, the producer who conceived the reunion idea, had delivered a blockbuster, one of the top ten Nielsen-rated shows of the week. He called me again with a brilliant new idea. "Would you be willing to re-create the shooting on television?" he asked.

"For a million dollars, David!" I said sarcastically. "I'll be happy to do it if someone wants to pay me that much. Otherwise, forget it." We hung up, and I never heard from him again.

Three weeks later I was in New York, appearing on *Good Morning America* on the fifteenth anniversary of the shooting. This had been, on the other hand, a very appealing offer because they were doing a piece called "Life after the Light" and wanted to talk about where I was in my life. I was actually in a terrific place and looking forward to saying so and hope-fully being an inspiration to people. Wouldn't you know it, as I was walking the streets in New York, a huge photo of Joey and Amy holding hands on the front page of the *New York Post* was suddenly in my face, on every newsstand on every street corner of the city. I absolutely could not believe my eyes. Apparently they were "back together." Both were divorcing their spouses and planned to live together. To say I was shocked was an understatement. This announcement made a big, but short-lived media splash as they appeared together on shows discussing their "reunion."

I was sure I knew what was going on here. David had conceived of this stunt and convinced these two boneheads that this would lead to all sorts of lucrative deals—probably their own reality show was the goal—and they would eventually both make tons of money. What he didn't count on was that no one cared. America was interested for about five minutes, then yawned and moved on. No one wanted to follow Joey and Amy around with cameras. No one particularly cared about their lives, together or not. It was a joke—but Jessica and Paul weren't laughing.

To see their father hugging, kissing, and holding hands on television with the woman who had almost killed their mother was the last straw for them. Joey's actions never ceased to surprise me, but I couldn't believe Amy would do this—she had two small children of her own. What kind of message was she sending? She was just like Joe in that she never knew when to shut her mouth, lie low, and go away. The two of them were made for each other, at least in that sense. Too bad nothing ever materialized. The story soon evaporated, no one divorced anyone, and everyone forgot the whole thing.

Everyone except for our family, of course. It was just one more embarrassing episode, the kind that had become all too familiar and would no doubt continue for the rest of our lives. Though I had yet to learn the clinical term for this kind of behavior, this latest stunt proved once and for all just exactly what we were up against: sociopathy. Joey Buttafuoco is a sociopath. And forever will be.

AFTERWORD

Father's Day 2007 was my "a-ha moment." Talk about the child teaching the parent. It was as if the lights suddenly came on. I felt like Helen Keller after she realized that the gestures her teacher Annie Sullivan kept making on her hands were words, and that words had a meaning. I'd spent decades trying to fix things . . . reading plenty of "How to Save Your Marriage" columns in women's magazines and scanning all the latest self-help books. In all that time, I never once heard the word "sociopath." Certainly, plenty of the things Joey did during our marriage made me crazy. I became increasingly angry, frustrated, and just plain fed up with my husband about his poor choices. But more than anything else, I was just plain baffled. I could not understand *why* he acted the way he did for so long. Why did he *never get it*?

The best answer I could come up with was that my former husband's refusal to "grow up" was the root of Joey's problem, the source of my misery, and the eventual cause of our divorce—that is, until our son introduced me to the word "sociopath." The best thing about this realization and all I've learned about this condition is the freedom I feel. I no longer blame myself, or even him, for all the events that went so wrong all through our lives together. I honestly believe the man can't help himself. He simply does not possess the emotional capacity to comprehend how his actions affect others. All the millions of words, excuses, and cajoling mean absolutely nothing. Finally accepting that reality has freed me to go on with my life with no more regrets and "what ifs."

So it is through different—wiser—eyes that I watch as Joey and Amy Fisher continue to make headlines. The year 2008 began with a surprise: Amy Fisher, whose name will be forever linked with mine, was back in the news because of a sex tape. *Amy Fisher Caught on Tape* was "private" footage taken by her husband, and at first she protested that he had released it without her knowledge. Soon enough, she was all over the national media promoting it. Not to be outdone, a couple of months later Joey and Evanka popped up claiming that they had been set up at a friend's house, in a guest room with hidden cameras. Their own graphic sex tape was soon all over the Internet, and the two of them made the rounds of talk shows protesting their innocence. I, for one, didn't buy their stories—any of them. *It wasn't their fault, they were set up, they had no idea* . . . I'd heard it all before, a thousand times.

So far, this year has been fairly quiet. Amy Fisher, now in her midthirties and the mother of three young children, has launched a new career as a high-end stripper/pole dancer. Joey and I have resumed talking on occasion. Given my newfound knowledge of sociopathic behavior, my emotional reactions to his antics have dwindled. Experts recommend that the only way to deal with a sociopath is to cut off all contact. However, that is not always possible, particularly when children are involved. I now possess the power to keep his behavior from affecting me. To this day, he tells me how sorry he is, how letting me get away was the biggest mistake of his life, how much he regrets everything, how much I still mean to him. He refers to heart-tugging memories of high school, or our honeymoon time in the little cottage, or one of the many old friends and good times we shared years ago.

But I take it all with a grain of salt, hang up the phone without a pang, and resume my daily life as stepmother to two adolescents in a *Brady Bunch*–style household. It's all about homework, curfews, chauffeuring, high school games, and family gatherings. And I have a solid partnership with Stu— barbecuing, going out to a dinner and a movie, watching our twenty-something kids navigate adulthood, and quietly sitting home after a full day's work, catching our favorite television shows. Is it routine? Yes! Am I content? Very! This is certainly not the life I expected, but it's the life I've earned and chosen for myself, and I wouldn't have it any other way.

ACKNOWLEDGMENTS

First and foremost, to my literary agent Sharlene Martin: Thanks for working so hard and believing in me when sometimes I didn't believe in myself. It only takes one! Julie McCarron, you went above and beyond the call of duty when you hooked up with me! Thank you from the bottom of my heart for all your hard work! My editor, Michele Matrisciani at HCI Books, for getting me and seeing the bigger picture. Kim Weiss, I'm glad I made your job a little easier!

To my family: My mom, Pat Connery, who taught me how to be strong by her own example and used humor in the face of adversity. My dad, Al Connery, who loved comedy and turned me on to Looney Tunes, Laurel and Hardy, George Carlin, Bill Cosby, Robert Klein, and Tiny Tim. And the New York Giants! I miss you every day. My little sisters, Jeanne, Kathy, Ellen, and Eileen, who drove me nuts as a little kid but are now a source of strength and laughter as we enter old age. Long live YouTube! I love that we can still laugh after all these years! My "other" brothers and sisters, Anne and Ken—your love and generosity know no bounds. I love you both so much and can't begin to thank you for all the love and support you have shown me throughout the years. Bobby and Ursula Buttafuoco: Bobby, you had to deal with as much as I did. Like me, you loved your brother with all your heart, but in the end, had to walk away. I know your pain, but I am so proud of you for making a beautiful life with Ursula and your children. Dad would be proud. Urs, ya did good! I love you! Bruce, thank you for being my "big brother" and for hanging out with me. I miss you. Luke, I wish things could have been different. Michael and Serena Sbarra, Chris and Dennis McCaully, thank you for your love and support. My nephews and niece, Cass, Alex, and Nicole. I missed you growing up, but am so proud of the young adults you have become. Richie and Joseph, Mom and Dad will tell you all about Aunt Mary Jo and Uncle Joey someday. Hang on to your hats! The Bennett family: Patty, Peggy, and Bonnie Sue, and their spouses and children, and their parents, Chuck and Joanne. We had some wonderful family functions together, and I will always remember them! My father-in-law, Cass, who didn't know that his son was a sociopath and tried with all his might and heart to make things right. I was proud to be your daughter-in-law. Willie Mae, now that I have stepchildren of my own, I can really appreciate the sacrifices you made when you took on the Buttafuoco children. You are a saint in my eyes! I miss you both very much. To all my aunts, uncles, and cousins, especially my cousin, Susan Hart. I will never forget you helping me out in the hospital when I was too weak to stand, walk, or brush my teeth or hair. I am so grateful for your love and support!

To my new family: Thelma Bernard, I can only imagine what you must have thought when your son said to you, "Mom, guess who I'm going out with? Mary Jo Buttafuoco!" You are such a wonderful woman, with a heart of gold. Thank you for accepting me into your family and for loving me. Mitch and Linda, my newest "big brother and little sister," you two are great, and I love you very much! To their children, Philip, Ryan, Christina, Jordan, Griffin, and Ethan, thanks for letting Paul, Jessica, and me be a part of your lives.

To my stepchildren, Martine, Cameron, and Hutton. Someday, when you are old and gray, you are going to remember me and say, "She was a pain in the ass, but other than the fact that she repeated herself constantly, she was a pretty cool lady!" I love you like my own.

Stuart, what can I say? You showed me, by example, what a man really is. I never thought that I could love someone again. Falling in love with you was a gift from God, and I am forever grateful that you came into my life.

Thank you to the staff at the Betty Ford Center for your dedication and perseverance in helping people overcome their addictions and in giving them the tools to lead a happy, fulfilling life. And to all the women who were with me during my stay there, I hope that you have all found peace and contentment in sobriety.

Massapequa and Massapequa Park were wonderful areas to grow up in. I was very blessed that my parents worked hard so that I could grow up in a wonderful community with so many fantastic people. My years at St. Rose of Lima Grammar School and Massapequa High School were what I wanted for my own children. Thank you to all the friends I made while I was growing up, especially Eileen Forte, Donna Abatemarco, Sue Hendershott, Patty and Kenny Von Glahn, John Barrett, Tom White, Jim Rice (who taught me how to drive and made me laugh a lot . . . A, I'm adorable!), my first real boyfriend, Tom Neillo (thought I'd forgotten about you, huh?), Mona Steinruck, Stew Gamper (who took care of me on the bus on my first day of kindergarten), and all the other kids on Kinsella Avenue: Michele, Denise and Nick Tardo, Ginny, Al, and Ken Schmadke. I remember when the snowplow would push all the snow up against the dead-end fence, and to us it was as big as any mountain in the Colorados! All the gang in the St. Rose of Lima Youth Group from the '70s (what a fun and innocent time in my life!). I learned how to play "A Horse with No Name" on the guitar!

My friends from "The Fort": Paul Myers, his brothers Gene and Denny, his sister Rickki, and their parents, Mr. and Mrs. Myers, thank you for putting up with a bunch of ragtag teenagers! Stephanie Salafrio, Joe Smith, Kathy Meyer (rest in peace), Jimmy Stanton (who, in sixth-grade science class, took one of the dead frogs and started singing, "Everybody Do the Michigan Rag!"). Noreen Jones, Tom Santry, and Rob Shaw (think how much easier my life would have been if I hadn't broken up with you and started dating Joey!). I know there are others who came into my life at this time; please forgive an old lady for not remembering all your names! Blame it on the weed and beer! Also, love and thanks to Robert Croes. There are two friends who will always stand out to me. They were my "best friends" at a time when life was simple and the biggest decision that needed to be made was what we were going to wear to school the next day: Terese McCarthy and Joanne Shields. With Terese, we used to put sweaters around our heads and pretend to be nuns, that is, when we weren't going around the neighborhood trying to adopt every stray animal we found! And Joanne and I always loved to play with our Barbie dolls. As teenagers, we would play with them in secret, so that all the other kids didn't think we were babies for still playing with dolls. Thank you, Terese, and God bless you in heaven, Joanne. Love also to Terry McGullam, John Beermann, and Suzanne Frasier.

Thank you to everyone who worked at Pathmark in Seaford when I was in high school. Bet you never could have guessed that this lowly cashier and her grocery-bagging boyfriend would one day be on the cover of the *New York Post* (a lot!).

Thanks also to Joan Lewis, Diane Roseberry, MaryEllen, Jeanne, Julianna, Rosemary, Diane, Sarah, and everybody else at National Bank of North America in the Huntington Quadrangle Offices. I hope your lives turned out a little less dramatic than mine!

A shout-out to Diane and Rich, Pat and Frank, Janet and Ed, Linda and Bob, and all of the teachers and friends from Giant Step nursery school and the saints who worked for and with United Cerebral Palsy of Nassau County. It was an honor to be involved with you. My bowling game has never been the same since we were all on a league together! Yes, Joey and I were on a bowling league . . .

I would probably not be here today without the heroic measures of the people who worked for the Nassau County Emergency Medical Trauma team on May 19, 1992. Thank you for being so selfless and for saving my life. You are true angels here on earth!

To the helicopter pilots who transported me to Nassau County Medical Center: I'm sorry I didn't remember the ride! My first time in a copter, and I missed it! Thank you for transporting me safely from the Biltmore Beach Club to the hospital.

To my friends and neighbors in Biltmore Shores: I want you to know how truly grateful I am to have had you in my life. The years I spent there before I got shot were truly the most wonderful times of my life. Your love and concern for me and my children was incredible. I wanted to stay there forever. Some of you have been lucky enough to stay, while others have moved on. To Josephine Slattery, you heard the shot. I remember you telling me that something didn't sound right, and you got up from the kitchen to look out the front door. You said that it was as if a force propelled you to go find out what that sound was. I know that God was pushing you that day. To Joe Slattery, thank you for listening to your wife when she insisted you go outside and find out why Mary

Jo was lying on a red blanket in front of the house. You were the first one to see that it wasn't a blanket I was lying on, but my own blood I was lying in.

To Joan and Frank Classi, MaryBeth and Bill Malloy, Joyce and Dan Farino, Joe and Karen Knight, Tom and Agatha Kelly, Tom and Carol Asher, Jean and Jim Purpura, Ray and Kim Bressingham, Steve and Patty Berringer, Doug and Regina Kaiser, Tom and Patty Burke, Marilyn and Ali Catik, Dave and Maria Hancock, June and Tony Carrarri, Bill and Nancy Schreck, Mike and Michele Ruiz, Lou and Fran Gigi, Laim and Joanne Maygothling, Joe and Andrea Widen, Roz and Sal Silippo, Peachy and Phil Giambanco, Mike and Madeline Salaba, the Basso Family, Jean and Henry, Carol, Barbara, and Pam, Tom Truglia, Paul and Colette Trupia, Sharon and Tom Marx, Janet and John Koons, Julie and Kevin McAndrews, Russ and Suzanne Javors, the LaGregas, the Finns, the Greismeyers, the Borgensons, the Dowells, the Tobins, and the Dursos: I can't thank you enough for all the love and support you gave us. We laughed and cried together through all of the insanity! Thank you also to my many other neighbors who took Paul and Jessie under their wings and tried to shield them from the constant barrage that was my life for far too long.

I would also like to thank Diane O'Brien and her family (at one point, going to see you was the only peace I had!). I'm glad we reconnected! Love that Facebook! Also, love to Sherri Spillane, Reed Anthony, Ron, Joann, and Vanessa Berlinsky,

Toni, Blair, and Carly Tardino, and the whole Tardino clan. I share a bond with you because we have all loved and been disappointed by Joey.

Thank you to Tim and Denise, Brett and Diane, Rick Perry, and all the gang who have been so nice and accepting of me when Tony Wood brought me around! And thank you, Tony, for looking back!

A special thank-you to Howard Stern, Robin Quivers, Artie Lange, Fred Norris, Gary Dell'Abate, Jackie Martling, Benjy Bronk, Sal Governale, Richard Christy, Scott Salem, J.D., Teddy, Mike, Will, Jason, Lisa G., Steve Langeford, Bob Levy, Shuli Egar, John Melendez, and to everyone who works or has worked on *The Howard Stern Show*. I'm proud to say I've been a fan for thirty years and a friend for seventeen years. You made a lot of unbearable days bearable with your humor and honesty. Thank you also to Dominic Barbara for being so wonderful and generous to me and my family. Also to Bruce Barket, who, as a lawyer and a religious man, is an anomaly to me (just kidding!). Maybe we were fooled, but it was only because our hearts were in the right place.

Words cannot express the gratitude that I feel for Dr. Babik Azizzadeh and his wife, Jessica. Thank you so much for everything you have done for me and my family. I came in as a patient and found lifelong friends. Thank you also to your staff for being so professional and kind. Thank you to Dr. Lance Wyatt, Dr. William Slattery from the House Ear

Institute, Dr. David Alessi, Dr. Babak Larian, Dr. Robert Sacks, and Dr. Jeremy Fine. Your generosity and kindness know no bounds. Thank you also to Theresa England, Nicholas Manley, the La Peer Surgical Center, St. Vincent's Medical Center, the House Clinic, the Beverly Tower Imaging Center, and the Serenity Aftercare Center.

ABOUT THE AUTHORS

After a five-year courtship and a twenty-five-year marriage to Joey Buttafuoco, **Mary Jo Buttafuoco** now lives quietly in Ventura County, California, with her fiancé, Stu, and their blended family.

Julie McCarron is a *New York Times* bestselling author and celebrity collaborator. Her works include Tracey Gold's *Room to Grow,* rocker Gene Simmons's *Sex, Money, Kiss,* and *Why I Love Baseball* with Larry King, among others.